For:

_____

From:

_____

I love thee with the breath,

Smiles, tears, of all my life!

—Elizabeth Barrett Browning

ACKNOWLEDGMENTS

100 Ways to Say I Love You. *Grand Rapids, MI: Zondervan, 1993.*

Barnes, Emilie. A Cup of God's Love. *Eugene, OR: Harvest House Publishers, 1999.*

Bell, Valerie. A Well-Tended Soul: Staying Beautiful for the Rest of Your Life. *Grand Rapids, MI: Zondervan, 1996.*

Boassy, Gal Talbott. A Romantic Treasury of Love. *Eugene, OR: Harvest House Publishers, 1999.*

Booher, Dianna. Love Notes From my Heart to Yours. *Nashville, TN: Word Publishing, a Division of Thomas Nelson, Inc., 1997.*

The Best of Ideals. *Nashville, TN: Ideals Publishing Corp., 1989.*

Chapin, Alice. 400 Creative Ways to Say I Love You. *Wheaton, IL: Tyndale House Publishers, Inc., 1996.*

Exley, Richard. Straight From the Heart for Couples. *Tulsa, OK: Honor Books, 1995.*

Favorite Hymns of Praise. *Wheaton, IL: Tabernacle Publishing Company, 1977.*

Gaither, Gloria. Bless This Marriage. *Nashville, TN: J. Countryman, a Division of Thomas Nelson, Inc., 1998.*

Godek, Gregory J. P. 10,000 Ways to Say I Love You. *Naperville, IL: Casablanca Press, a Division of Sourcebooks, Inc., 1999.*

God's Little Instruction Book for Couples. *Tulsa, OK: Honor Books, 1995.*

God's Little Instruction Book on Love. *Tulsa, OK: Honor Books, 1996.*

Gonring, Colleen Callahan, ed. Ideals Valentine. *Milwaukee, WI: Ideals Publishing Corporation, 1982.*

Hewett, James S. Illustrations Unlimited. *Wheaton, IL: Tyndale House Publishers, Inc., 1988.*

Jarrell, Jane C. 26 Ways to Say "I Love You." *Eugene, OR: Harvest House Publishers, 2000.* 31 Ideas for Spreading Love at Lunch. *Eugene, OR: Harvest House Publishers, 2000.* Love You Can Touch. *Eugene, OR: Harvest House Publishers, 1999.*

McDonald, Marge, and Richard J. Lenz. Simple Wisdom of Love. *Atlanta, GA: Longstreet Press, Inc., a Division of Cox Enterprises, Inc., 1999.*

Merrill, Dean. How to Really Love Your Wife. *Grand Rapids, MI: Zondervan, 1977.*

Osborne, Cecil G. How to Have a Happier Wife. *Grand Rapids, MI: Zondervan, 1970.*

Penwell, Dan. 101 Things to Do in the Year 2000. *Tulsa, OK: Honor Books, 1999.*

Sanna, Ellyn, writer/compiler. The Language of the Heart. *Uhrichsville, OH: Barbour Publishing, Inc., 1999.*

Smalley, Gary. How to Become Your Husband's Best Friend. *Grand Rapids, MI: Zondervan, 1982.*

Tada, Joni Eareckson. God's Precious Love. *Grand Rapids, MI: Zondervan, 1998.*

Weaver, Joanna. With This Ring. *Colorado Springs, CO: WaterBrook Press, 1999.*

Wheeler, Susan. We Belong Together. *Eugene, OR: Harvest House Publishers, 2001.*

1001

WAYS TO SAY

I LOVE YOU

An inspirational collection of loving
ideas for the *woman* in your life

Ψ
inspirio™
The gift group of Zondervan

INTRODUCTION

We talk a lot about love, but when it comes to living love, we sometimes lack original ideas to show our feelings to the folks we love the most. This lighthearted, fun-filled book can help with practical ideas for showing your love in big and little ways. You'll find more than mere suggestions for your to-do list with:

- "A Time to Remind"—take time to do something that shows your love
- "A Chance for Romance"—suggestions to ignite the fires of love
- "Let Me Count the Ways"—lists of reasons for loving someone
- "Love N Cents"—inexpensive things to do, give, or say to share your love
- "Loving Words"—God's words and inspirational insights about love from the NIV Bible.

In all, there are 1001 ways to rekindle a romantic mindset. And, if you put one idea into practice each day, that's almost three years of ways to say *I love you!*

This compilation also comes with a built-in twist. Half of the book contains suggestions for him, then flip the book over, end-over-end, and you'll find suggestions for her. Let this delightful, innovative book get you started showing your love to that someone special—in 1001 ways—and more.

A TIME TO REMIND

Take the time to remind her you love her when you:

- Bake her favorite cookies.
- Squirrel away some extra money and surprise her with a gift certificate to her favorite store.
- Help her balance her checkbook without getting angry.
- Take her to her favorite restaurant.
- Read and learn about her favorite hobby or sport.
- Write her a love letter and send it to her work address.
- Give her a day away from the kids.
- Listen to her share about her day without interrupting.
- Vacuum the carpet without being asked.
- Volunteer to do a chore you know she dislikes.
- Be yourself.

- Go for long walks together.
- Be patient with each other.
- Write "I Love You" on a sticky note and put it in the silverware drawer.
- Say you are sorry.
- Clean out the bathroom sink when you're done.
- Be nice to her mother.
- Let her have all of her friends over.
- Give her a Saturday off.
- Share a juicy apple.
- Hang her picture in your office.
- Hang up your clothes, towel, coat, etc., after you're finished with them.
- Cuddle together in front of the fireplace, not the TV.
- Listen.
- Leave her a sexy message on the answering machine.
- Buy her favorite candy bar for her.
- Willingly watch her try on outfits in the mall for at least two hours.
- Don't leave toothpaste spit on the mirror.
- Share her dreams.
- Tell her you're glad you married her.
- Let her drive.
- Turn off the TV in the middle of a football game.
- Surprise her with a kiss in public.
- Bring home flowers unexpectedly.
- Change one of your bad habits.

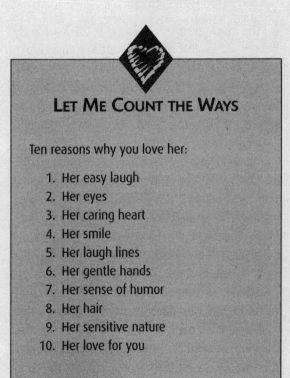

LET ME COUNT THE WAYS

Ten reasons why you love her:

1. Her easy laugh
2. Her eyes
3. Her caring heart
4. Her smile
5. Her laugh lines
6. Her gentle hands
7. Her sense of humor
8. Her hair
9. Her sensitive nature
10. Her love for you

CELEBRATE THE ORDINARY

In the most unexpected places, at the least likely times, life in all of its multi-faceted splendor broke upon us. Once it happened to Brenda and me while we were eating Church's chicken sitting cross-legged on the floor of the living room with our backs against a roll of carpet. Even now, as I write about it, something of the feeling comes back.

Night and day, for the better part of three weeks, we had worked to renovate that rundown rental house and finally it was starting to feel like home. Swallowing one last bite of chicken, I leaned back against the roll of carpet and wiped my hands on my soiled jeans. It was a rare moment—a true serendipity, and I felt fulfilled in a deeply satisfying way.

Looking at Brenda I suddenly realized how blessed I was. She had committed herself to me, holding nothing back. Without a complaint, she had followed me from one struggling church to another. She was my closest friend and lover, the mother of my only child.

That afternoon, she was wearing jeans and a T-shirt. Her hair was a mess and there was a smudge of paint on her cheek. Still, she had never looked better, and I loved her more than I can say.

From somewhere down the street the sound of children's laughter drifted through our open window. In the distance a dog barked, and belatedly I realized that God was with us. I'm not sure where that thought came from, but suddenly it was there. In a strange sort of way, that unfinished living room became a sanctuary; chicken and corn-on-the-cob, a holy meal; and our conversation a kind of prayer.

Even now, more than twenty years later, the memory of that moment has the power to transfix me. The wonder of life and love transcends the monotony of our days. In truth, the best marriages are made of moments like that. Moments when the simple joy of sharing life with the one you love transfuses all of life with a kind of haunting beauty.

RICHARD EXLEY

I love you!

- Rent a tuxedo and take her to McDonald's for lunch.
- Forgive her.
- Listen to her favorite kind of music without complaint.
- Give hugs and kisses often.
- Eat a snack together and enjoy the quiet time.
- Leave a loving message on a sticky note over the kitchen sink.
- Watch a romantic movie.
- Keep a picture of the two of you in plain sight.
- Always kiss goodbye.
- Tuck a love note in her purse.
- Send her a romantic card every day for a week.
- Take time to laugh together.
- Give her a foot massage.
- Play a game together.
- Become her best friend.
- Bring home her favorite takeout food.
- Tell her five reasons why you love her.
- Turn off the phone, TV, and pager and make her your top priority for an entire evening.
- Unconditionally accept her.
- Offer to do one of her chores.
- Compromise cheerfully when necessary.
- View your spouse as God's gift to you.
- Value the things she values.
- Stay open to her feedback and don't become defensive.
- Thank God for your differences—and mean it!

A CHANCE FOR ROMANCE

A small gesture of affection may be all that's needed to communicate a loving, caring heart to your beloved. See how many of these small suggestions you can incorporate into your relationship this week and watch the spark of romance rekindle and burn brightly:

When walking about in public, reach for her hand as you did when you first started courting.

Show some chivalry in your attention by offering your arm as you cross a street, standing when she enters the room, holding the door for her, or opening and closing her car door for her.

Look for ways to make her feel special—give her a timely, specific compliment, take notice of her hair style or dress, gently caress her cheek with the back of your hand.

In these simple ways you can assure the woman you love that she is special, and that assurance is an important part of romance.

I love you!

- Say "no" to an outing with the guys or a sporting event, and spend the day with her instead.
- Watch a sunset together.
- Buy a new hat to replace the grungy cap you know she dislikes.
- Smile every time you see her.
- Pray for her.
- Get rid of your faded, ripped flannel shirt, even though it's comfortable.
- Serenade her with your special song.
- Be impetuous and impractical.
- Wear her favorite after shave lotion.
- Let her take you to an art museum, and really try to enjoy it.
- Give up your activities with the guys for one week and give her your attention instead.
- Develop a shared interest, activity, or sport.
- Share secrets together.
- Make her your top priority.
- Remember the first time you said, "I love you" to each other.
- Run an errand she hates to do.
- Stay in bed and cuddle.
- Believe in her.
- Leave love notes in the refrigerator.
- Care about what has happened in her day.
- Convince her to do something adventurous— just with you.
- Make the coffee the way she likes it.
- Be understanding.
- Laugh at the jokes she tells—even if she ruins the punch line.

MR. FIX IT

Put on your tool belt; wire up those power tools; your relationship needs some work!

According to Virginia Satir, hugs are essential for human development: "Our pores are places for messages of love and physical contact. Four hugs a day are necessary for survival, eight for maintenance, and twelve for growth."

As "Mr. Fix It," your task today is to make sure your sweetie's pores are getting all the growth they need. Begin with two gentle hugs, just to get things warmed up. Allow the pores to cool between hugs.

Make the next two hugs surprise hugs. Remember, these are her "survival" hugs.

The next four hugs can come in quick succession or be spaced throughout the day. By this time the "hugger" should begin to see some warmth from the "huggee."

Before the day is over, make sure you've given the last four hugs. Now you can congratulate yourself, Mr. Fix It. You've restored some weakened pores (both *hers* and *yours*) to health once again!

I love you!

LOVING WORDS

Live a life of love, just as Christ loved us and gave himself up for us as a fragrant offering and sacrifice to God.

Ephesians 5:2

Mercy, peace and love be yours in abundance.

Jude 2

You are forgiving and good, O Lord, abounding in love to all who call to you.

Psalm 86:5

Be completely humble and gentle; be patient, bearing with one another in love. Make every effort to keep the unity of the Spirit through the bond of peace.

Ephesians 4:2–3

- Learn a new dance step together.
- Place a love note under the windshield wiper of her car.
- Pick up one of her favorite snack foods the next time you're at the gas station.
- Give her a back rub.
- Send her flowers.
- Leave her a romantic message on her e-mail.
- Hold her favorite candy bar in your teeth and offer her a bite.
- Send her a note to say thanks for being your soul mate.
- Buy season tickets to the local theatre—and go together!
- Go to the symphony together.

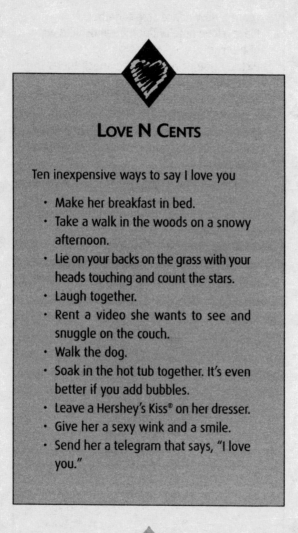

LOVE N CENTS

Ten inexpensive ways to say I love you

- Make her breakfast in bed.
- Take a walk in the woods on a snowy afternoon.
- Lie on your backs on the grass with your heads touching and count the stars.
- Laugh together.
- Rent a video she wants to see and snuggle on the couch.
- Walk the dog.
- Soak in the hot tub together. It's even better if you add bubbles.
- Leave a Hershey's Kiss® on her dresser.
- Give her a sexy wink and a smile.
- Send her a telegram that says, "I love you."

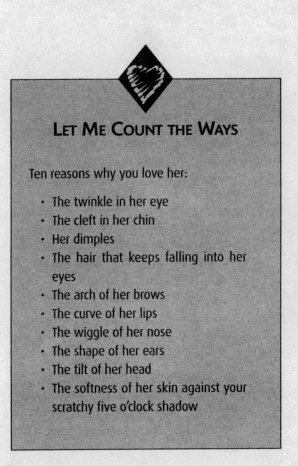

LET ME COUNT THE WAYS

Ten reasons why you love her:

- The twinkle in her eye
- The cleft in her chin
- Her dimples
- The hair that keeps falling into her eyes
- The arch of her brows
- The curve of her lips
- The wiggle of her nose
- The shape of her ears
- The tilt of her head
- The softness of her skin against your scratchy five o'clock shadow

Love is the one business in which it pays to be an absolute spendthrift: Give it away; throw it away; splash it over; empty your pockets; share the basket; and tomorrow you'll have more than ever.

God gives us each other, and the tools for cultivating our blessed oneness, but it is up to us to work the soil of our relationship all the days of our lives.

RICHARD EXLEY

LOVE SONNETS

First give me one kiss, and to that kiss a score,
Then to that twenty, add a hundred more,
A thousand to that hundred, so kiss on,
To make that thousand up a million.
Treble that million, and when that is done,
Let's kiss afresh, as when we first begun.

ROBERT HERRICK

I love thee, I love but thee,
with a love that shall not die
Till the sun grows cold, and the stars are old,
And the leaves of the Judgment Book unfold.

BAYARD TAYLOR

I love you!

- Never say anything negative about her to anyone else.
- Make up your own nicknames for each other.
- Take turns reading aloud together from a favorite book.
- Don't rearrange her kitchen cupboards to make them more efficient.
- Give her a surprise party just because you love her.
- Look for ways to share her load.
- Don't try to buy her clothes—give her a gift certificate instead and let her buy her own!
- Let her mother advise you.
- Watch her and listen to her to find out what really interests her.
- Participate in her hobbies.
- Take some time to talk seriously about your relationship—but not when her favorite drama is on.
- Surprise her with tickets to the ballet for her and a friend.
- Don't keep a record of how many times you've done the things she wants to do.
- Learn to ride a horse together.
- Use every opportunity to applaud her.
- Let her channel surf with the remote control at least once a day without complaint.
- Remember that a way to a woman's heart is through romance.

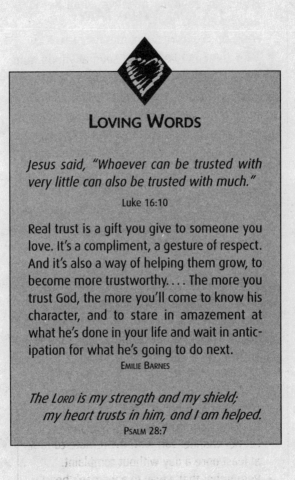

LOVING WORDS

Jesus said, "Whoever can be trusted with very little can also be trusted with much."
Luke 16:10

Real trust is a gift you give to someone you love. It's a compliment, a gesture of respect. And it's also a way of helping them grow, to become more trustworthy.... The more you trust God, the more you'll come to know his character, and to stare in amazement at what he's done in your life and wait in anticipation for what he's going to do next.
EMILIE BARNES

The LORD is my strength and my shield; my heart trusts in him, and I am helped.
PSALM 28:7

COME WHAT MAY

Kim Carpenter had never seen anything more beautiful in his life. Teal ribbon and pink roses line the candlelit chapel where he and 250 guests stood. But Kim saw only his bride. A stab of pure joy pierced his heart as Krickitt met him at the altar, her incredible blue eyes mirroring the excitement and love in his own eyes.

Every detail of the ceremony is seared into Kim's memory. But of that day several years ago Krickitt remembers nothing. The wedding is gone—wiped from Krickitt's memory by the nearly fatal car crash she and Kim were in just ten weeks after their wedding. Gone as well are the memories of her and Kim's courtship, love, and marriage.

The doctors put Krickitt's chance of survival at less than 1 percent, but people began to pray. Ten days after the accident, Krickitt started to regain consciousness.

Questions followed. Some Krickitt answered right, others wrong. But when asked, "Who's your husband?" Krickitt paused a moment, then said, "I'm not married."

It was a blow Kim will never forget.

After many months, Krickitt finally moved home. But nothing was the same. Kim says, "We had to start over." And start over they did. They began dating again. He had wooed her once, and Kim was determined to win her again. "I had said my vows before God—'in sickness and in health'—and I meant them."

As for Krickitt: "I knew that if I loved him before, God could help me love him again."

Finally, on Valentine's Day, 1996, three years after the accident, Kim proposed once again. Krickitt accepted.

The ceremony was simple, yet sacred. Each after the other, they repeated the vows that had held them together. Vows that had been tested by fire and found true.

JOANNA WEAVER

I love you!

A TIME TO REMIND

Take a moment to remind her of the reasons you fell in love with her:

- The way she took your hand
- The way she said, "Good night"
- Her concern for your pets
- Her understanding heart
- Her giving nature
- Her ability to see the good things in you
- Her trust in you
- Her love for others
- Her love for God
- Her uncompromising honesty

LET ME COUNT THE WAYS

Ten reasons why you love her:

- She makes you laugh.
- She makes you smile.
- She makes you feel all warm inside.
- She makes you feel dizzy.
- She makes you feel crazy.
- She makes you snicker.
- She makes you groan.
- She makes you comfortable.
- She makes you feel special.
- She makes you waffles.

- Always be her biggest fan.
- Give her a neck and shoulder massage after work.
- Enjoy studying the Bible together.
- Give up wearing your baseball cap in public if she asks you to.
- Smell good for her.
- Keep the passion between you so alive that channel surfing is seldom thought of as fulfilling entertainment.
- Thank her for all she does for you.
- Encourage her to be a leader.
- Squirrel away some money to surprise her with something she would like.
- Serve her needs, because we all want our needs to be met.
- Ask to go shopping with her.
- Give her the gift of a cheerful disposition.
- Put in the "Sleepless in Seattle" or "Princess Bride" video and watch it together.
- Let her have some time alone.
- Find ways to laugh together.
- Talk about what is troubling you with her first.
- Spend more time with her than with your car or truck.
- Be thankful in your heart for her.

MR. FIX IT

Mr. Fix It's skills are needed in the romance department. Put on your tool belt and arm yourself with a sharpened pencil, a clipboard, and clean paper. Now, write your beloved a love song—the words don't have to rhyme; it doesn't have to be long. But it does have to express how you feel about her.

When you've finished the song, here's the next step. Using calligraphy tools, paintbrushes, or a set of permanent markers, inscribe the lyrics on a scroll made of parchment paper. Burn and blacken the edges of the scroll just a bit with a lit match. Then frame the scroll in a shadow box frame and present it to your sweetheart as an "unbirthday" or "just because" present. The tears she'll shed will be tears of joy. And she'll love you for the time you've spent to tell her and everyone else who will see the frame how special this lady is to you.

I love you!

A Chance for Romance

To rekindle or keep the fires of romance burning in your relationship, why not recreate your first date or the first time you got together and realized that you liked each other. Set aside some time to go back to the same place and the same spot if possible. If the building or restaurant or location no longer exists or has changed hands, plan this rendezvous for as nearby as possible or in as similar a setting.

Remember as many things as you can about that date and approximate them again. What did the place look like? What music was playing in the background? What did it smell like? Was it crowded or just the two of you? Was it daytime or nighttime?

What did you have to eat and drink? What did you wear? What did you talk about? How did you get there?

See how many pieces of your first date you can recall and put together. Then, let your sweetie know that you have a wonderful place to go for a date and surprise her with this memory and chance for romance.

There are some people with such a lofty conception of love that they never succeed in expressing it in the simple kindnesses of ordinary life.

PAUL TOURNIER

Nothing beats love at first sight except love with insight.

If love is a jigsaw puzzle, falling in love is finding the corners.

I am two fools I know,
for loving, and for saying so.

JOHN DONNE

Diamonds may be forever, but nothing touches the heart like a love letter.

RICHARD EXLEY

Love does not consist in gazing at each other but in looking outward together in the same direction.

ANTOINE DE SAINT-EXUPERY

- Attend church together.
- Put down the paper and talk about your day with her.
- Take a walk together and don't talk—just hold hands and enjoy each other's company.
- Let her sit in your favorite chair for a change.
- Get her a small snow blower that she can operate when you're not around to shovel the driveway.
- Share an umbrella on a rainy day.
- Let her name the pets with cute names like "Fluffy" or "Sweetums."
- Go shopping where she wants without making a single negative comment.
- Bring home flowers unexpectedly.
- Let her win a snowball fight.
- Change the sheets on the bed.
- Go to "Stars on Ice" together instead of the ice hockey game.
- Get up with the kids or pets and let her sleep in.
- Let her drive.
- Don't assume that she feels loved—tell her and show her often.
- Wash the windows.
- If you don't like the outfit she's wearing, buy her another one.
- Wear in public the first handmade anything she makes for you—whether it's a sweater with the arms to your knees or a scarf that would fit the Jolly Green Giant.
- Massage her hands and feet.
- Clean out the bathroom sink after you've shaved.
- Don't wear T-shirts that don't cover your belly button.

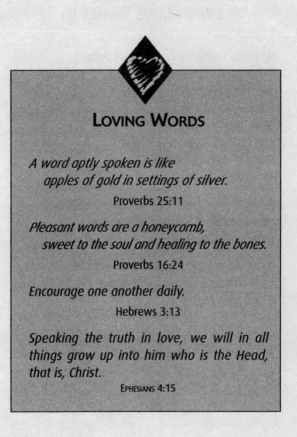

LOVING WORDS

*A word aptly spoken is like
    apples of gold in settings of silver.*

Proverbs 25:11

*Pleasant words are a honeycomb,
    sweet to the soul and healing to the bones.*

Proverbs 16:24

Encourage one another daily.

Hebrews 3:13

Speaking the truth in love, we will in all things grow up into him who is the Head, that is, Christ.

EPHESIANS 4:15

WHEN LOVE SHINES IN

How the world will grow with beauty,
When love shines in,
And the heart rejoice in duty,
When love shines in.
Trials may be sanctified,
And the soul in peace abide,
Life will all be glorified,
When love shines in.

When love shines in, when love shines in ...
How the heart is tuned to singing,
When love shines in.

When love shines in, when love shines in ...
Joy and peace to others bringing,
When love shines in.

MRS. FRANK A. BRECK

A TIME TO REMIND

Take time to remind her that you love her by looking up the meaning of her name in the back of an unabridged dictionary or in a baby names book. Make a plaque or a poster, etch a stained glass window panel, carve a wooden nameplate and take a photo of it, or in some other way make something permanent that will remind you both of her name and its significance.

Then, whenever you call her by name, remember the meaning behind that name. Reflect on the qualities hidden in that meaning. Picture her fulfilling the meaning of her name. Be proud of her and call to her attention those times when she lives up to her name and calling.

LOVING HER

Use this page to record your feelings about your love for her:

_____

_____

_____

_____

_____

_____

_____

_____

_____

_____

_____

_____

_____

_____

_____

_____

_____

_____

_____

_____

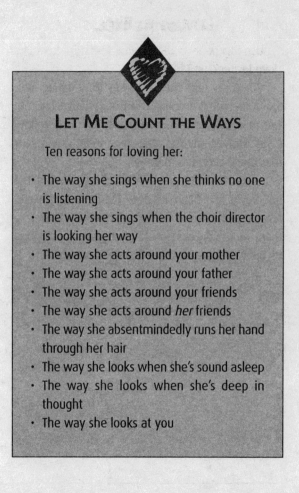

LET ME COUNT THE WAYS

Ten reasons for loving her:

- The way she sings when she thinks no one is listening
- The way she sings when the choir director is looking her way
- The way she acts around your mother
- The way she acts around your father
- The way she acts around your friends
- The way she acts around *her* friends
- The way she absentmindedly runs her hand through her hair
- The way she looks when she's sound asleep
- The way she looks when she's deep in thought
- The way she looks at you

LOVING TO EXCESS

Joni Eareckson Tada writes:

"When my husband Ken and I were dating, one word marked the expression of his love for me: Excessive. I received more vases of fresh yellow roses, stuffed animals, sweetheart-cards, and candies than I care to remember.

"I pleaded with him to lighten up, but I learned that not only is love blind, it's deaf. The next day I would receive pink roses instead of yellow ones. There are many more solid evidences of Ken's love I could point to, but it was the excesses that delighted me."

What are some of the things the love of your life enjoys? Candy, roses, cards? Perfume, china tea cups, puppy posters?

Or is she more interested in the outdoors, sporting events, or road rallies? Quilt shows, museums, or the symphony?

Follow Ken Tada's example and show how much you love your beloved by sharing these things with her to excess. For example, if she loves china tea cups, buy her a different cup and saucer each day for a week. End the week with a date for tea at an old world style hotel. Let your imagination go and excessively show your love to your beloved.

I love you!

LOVE N CENTS

Make yourself a "Love Box." You might want to use an old envelope or Kleenex box, a box you put together with scraps of wood, or a clean container from the hardware store. Decorate the container with a collage of snapshots of your special lady.

Keep the Love Box in a special place—out of sight of prying eyes, but near enough that you can access it quickly and easily. Then, whenever your sweetie does something wonderful, something that makes you thankful for her, something that warms your heart—no matter how big or small—write it down and tuck it into the Love Box.

After a specified time—a year, maybe, or on your anniversary or when she needs a real pick-me-up—pull out the Love Box and read the things you've written down together. She'll be able to see herself through your eyes as you remember lots of reasons why you love her.

- Hold hands when standing in line.
- Slip a love note into the pocket of her jeans.
- Pray for her every day.
- Have your picture taken professionally and put the photo in a unique frame just for her.
- Keep a scrapbook of just you two and the things you do together.
- Go ballroom dancing together.
- Write a letter to her mother and thank her for raising such a wonderful daughter.
- Send an "unbirthday" card.
- Give her a kind word or compliment.
- Look beyond the embarrassment of something that happens so that you can laugh together.
- Give her a peck on the cheek in a crowded elevator and tell her you love her.
- Rent a stretch limo for a few hours on her birthday and drive past her friends' homes.
- Be the first to say "I'm sorry."
- Love her so much that romance novels could be written about you.
- Give her a monogrammed blanket that you can use to snuggle in.
- Believe her when she says, "I wouldn't connect those two wires if I were you."
- Know when your "five-minute-project" has taken four hours, it's time to call the plumber.
- Plan to grow old together.
- Remember the date of the first time you said, "I love you," and let that warmth fill your heart again.

- Shelter her when she cries but don't try to "fix" the problem unless she asks for help. She may just want the comfort of your strong arms.
- Remember the promises you've made to her—whether marriage vows or otherwise—and keep them.
- Plan time to give to the community together—at a homeless shelter, serving food in a mission kitchen, or helping in a food distribution program.
- Like the shirt she bought you.
- Take out the trash without her asking you.
- Listen to her when she offers helpful criticisms.
- Take the old refrigerator to the dump instead of leaving it in the garage until you can fix it "someday."
- Clean out your closet before you clean out the garage.
- Ask her what she would like to do for your next vacation—and cheerfully do it.
- Hug more than you talk.
- Find an unexplored path and explore it together.
- Buy her "toys" before you buy yours.
- Never, never, never give a vacuum cleaner as a Valentine's Day gift.
- Don't laugh when she cries over a McDonald's commercial—hug her instead.
- Let her win the "tickle" war.
- Compliment her father.
- Don't be such a baby when you are sick.
- Help undecorate the house after Christmas.
- Leave the silly stuffed animal on your dash where she tucked it.

AN OLD-FASHIONED LOVE SONG

Wander the web, haunt a library, browse in a music store, paw through a box of old LP's, and see if you can locate the words and music to one of these old-fashioned love songs. Listen to it, learn it, and sing it to your beloved. Your voice may not be ready for the Met, but your voice is the one your beloved wants to hear singing a heartfelt song of love. Here are some titles to find:

"I'll Be Seeing You," Bing Crosby
"All of Me," Billie Holiday
"Smoke Gets in Your Eyes," The Platters
"Unforgettable," Nat King Cole
"Chances Are," Johnny Mathis
"Our Love is Here to Stay," George Gershwin

I love you!

Sharing the housework makes it easier to share the love.

Love thou, and if thy love be deep as mine, thou wilt not laugh at poets.

EDWARD BULWER-LYTTON

Love is not won—a reward for performance or achievement. You don't have to sing, teach, preach, or pray well to be loved. People will not love us for what we do but rather for what we are.

RANDY SPENCER

Passion is the quickest to develop, and the quickest to fade. Intimacy develops more slowly, and commitment more gradually still.

ROBERT STERNBERG

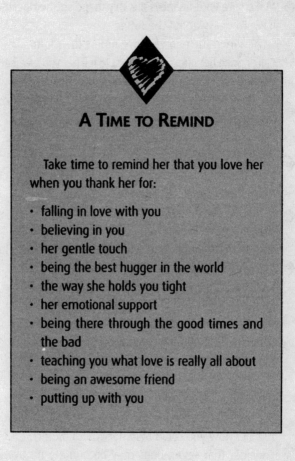

A TIME TO REMIND

Take time to remind her that you love her when you thank her for:

- falling in love with you
- believing in you
- her gentle touch
- being the best hugger in the world
- the way she holds you tight
- her emotional support
- being there through the good times and the bad
- teaching you what love is really all about
- being an awesome friend
- putting up with you

- Make sure your finances are shipshape so she doesn't have to worry about the future.
- Smile when the one you love enters the room.
- Call or page her unexpectedly just to tell her you love her.
- Change something in your decorating scheme to show her you care—move her picture by your chair; put her favorite stuffed animal in a prominent location, etc.
- Call a local radio station and dedicate a song to her.
- When she calls you at work, *always* interrupt whatever you're doing to concentrate on her call—don't even check the stock report on the Internet!
- Decorate the house with balloons—one for every month you've known her.
- Turn to her in public and whisper, "On a scale of 1 to 10, you're a 12!"
- Kiss the palm of her hand, close her fingers into a fist, and say, "Save this!"
- Give her a shopping spree—just for the fun of it.
- Don't expect anything back when you give her a nice dinner out.
- Live happily ever after.
- Believe in each other.
- Use one of your pet names for her as your ATM password.
- Ask her how you could help her with a project.
- Consider that seven dogs may be going a bit overboard for companionship.
- Love God first—then loving her will come naturally.

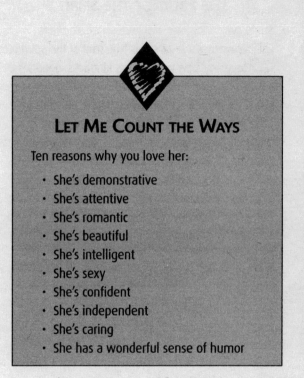

LET ME COUNT THE WAYS

Ten reasons why you love her:

- She's demonstrative
- She's attentive
- She's romantic
- She's beautiful
- She's intelligent
- She's sexy
- She's confident
- She's independent
- She's caring
- She has a wonderful sense of humor

THE FRUIT OF THE SPIRIT

Galatians 5:22–23 says: "The fruit of the Spirit is love, joy, peace, patience, kindness, goodness, faithfulness, gentleness and self-control." Notice that love is the first fruit mentioned. That's because love is the key to all of the other fruit of the Spirit.

About these verses, Donald Grey Barnhouse observed, "Love is the key. Joy is love singing. Peace is love resting. Long-suffering (patience) is love enduring. Kindness is love's touch. Goodness is love's character. Faithfulness is love's habit. Gentleness is love's self-forgetfulness. Self-control is love holding the reins."

May your love exhibit all the fruit of the Spirit in all its facets!

- Remember chivalry is **not** dead. Open the door for her; help her on with her coat; be a gentleman.
- Learn the art of giving a massage.
- Sing your special song to each other.
- Talk about the songs that have meant a lot to you over the years.
- Share prayer needs with each other.
- Talk about the differences and similarities in your faith and worship styles.
- Go to Sunday school together.
- Tell her about a dream or goal you would like to one day achieve.
- Ask her what her favorite color is.
- Ask her what she most likes to eat.
- Ask her where she would most like to live.
- Ask her what she would most like to do if money were no object.
- Don't just bring home "guilt" flowers—surprise her with spontaneous "posies" like dandelions, daisies, or a grocery store bouquet.
- Take her with you to go back and visit your birthplace.
- Buy her favorite flavor of seedless jam.
- Spend an afternoon in a used book store and look for a book you can read aloud to each other.
- Concentrate on communicating with her in more open ways 50 percent better than you did last week.

A Chance for Romance

Flowers are nice, a telephone call is wonderful, but when it comes to expressing the heart's deepest feelings, nothing is more effective than a letter. As one husband so aptly put it: "I could have called. It would have been far less trouble, but I would not have put the thought and effort into a call that I put into a letter. Besides, it would have been over in a matter of minutes. The letter she can keep for a lifetime."

He was right. A telephone call is wonderful, but it does not have the lasting impact of a letter written from the heart. When it's over, all you have is a warm feeling and a swiftly fading memory. A letter, on the other hand, can be kept and read again and again, warming the heart each time.

Virtually every woman has a collection of old love letters stored away in a drawer somewhere or in a trunk in the attic. They afford her the opportunity to relive the joys of courtship and romance for a lifetime. They remain, as always, love's most enduring expression.

RICHARD EXLEY

THE TEN COMMANDMENTS OF LOVE

- Treat her with strength and gentleness.
- Give ample praise and reassurance.
- Avoid criticism.
- Remember the importance of "little things."
- Recognize her need for togetherness.
- Give her a sense of security.
- Recognize the validity of her moods.
- Cooperate with her.
- Discover her particular needs.
- Try to meet those needs.

CECIL OSBORNE

A good marriage is like a casserole, only those responsible for it really know what goes in it.

Creation of woman from the rib of man: She was not made from his head to top him; nor out of his feet to be trampled upon by him; but out of his side to be equal with him, under his arm to be protected, and near his heart to be loved.

MATTHEW HENRY

LOVING WORDS

"As a bridegroom rejoices over his bride, so God rejoices over you" (Isaiah 62:5). That's stupendous. Incredible. There aren't enough adjectives to describe the wonder.

God bursts with joy over you. He observes your obeying him and exclaims, "Oh, joy!" And he will one day crown you with such joy everlasting.

JONI EARECKSON TADA

Why not share this wonderful insight with your beloved? Introduce her to the God of rejoicing!

MR. FIX IT

Fixing communication with your sweetheart takes as much work as fixing a set of brakes on your pickup. The most unfortunate thing about broken communication is that "its absence doesn't cause immediate repercussions. Your stomach doesn't growl as it does when you miss a meal." But if you're convinced that you need her and she needs you, then you'll find the time to fix your communication skills. Here are some suggestions of times to try and talk together:

Driving—a beautiful time for talking about all kinds of things. You're sitting there together and you can't do much else, so why not get in some quality time with each other. Even the short runs to shopping centers or to friends' houses are good opportunities to talk.

Restaurants—the big splashy ones, yes, but also the corner coffee shops where you can get two pecan rolls and two cups of coffee and sit for an hour if you like.

Vacations—the point of a vacation is not only to *do* some neat things and *avoid* the old grind, but also to *be with* each other for greater chunks of time than is possible in the normal week. Vacations are great for getting into those heavy topics that otherwise take too long.

Appointments—if the above situations aren't enough, there's nothing wrong with blocking out a certain hour each week simply to sit down together in the living room, turn off the TV, and talk.

Remember, Mr. Fix It can fix it. With a little creativity, energy, time, and planning you can put your communication skills back on track. Cut out the excuses. Get to work. It will be worth the effort.

ADAPTED FROM DEAN MERRILL

I love you!

- Organize a "Just Because I Love You" party with her friends and family.
- Order pizza for her and have it delivered to her office when she has to work late.
- Help her conquer one of her fears.
- Send a thank you card to her every day for an entire week; be specific in your gratitude.
- Encourage her to play an instrument for you.
- Help her break one bad habit this year.
- Give her one sincere compliment every day for a week.
- Be forgiving.
- Be intimate without having sex.
- Spend more time with her than you do watching sports.
- Spend more time with her than surfing on the web.
- Make a greeting card as tall as the room that says "I love you."
- Hold a contest to see who can be more romantic—you or her.
- Revisit your old high school together and share some of your memories with her.
- Visit a national park together and learn about its significance.
- Memorize each other's favorite passage of Scripture.

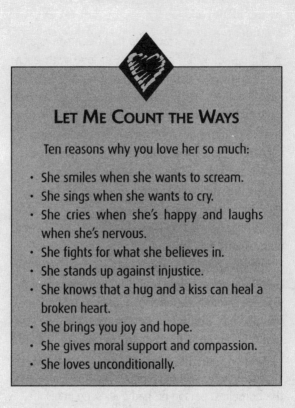

LET ME COUNT THE WAYS

Ten reasons why you love her so much:

- She smiles when she wants to scream.
- She sings when she wants to cry.
- She cries when she's happy and laughs when she's nervous.
- She fights for what she believes in.
- She stands up against injustice.
- She knows that a hug and a kiss can heal a broken heart.
- She brings you joy and hope.
- She gives moral support and compassion.
- She loves unconditionally.

AN INTERNET ROMANCE

A man and a woman who had been corresponding solely by e-mail fell in love with each other and decided to meet. Because they lived in different cities, they agreed to meet in an airport midway between their two homes. They had never seen each other, nor sent each other photographs of each other, so they devised a way to help them recognize each other. Since it was still wintertime they agreed that she would wear a green hat and a green scarf. He would tuck a green carnation in his coat lapel. They decided upon a day to meet and waited with curious anticipation.

The man's flight was a bit delayed, so he knew that the woman would probably be there before he was. He carefully fastened the green carnation onto his top coat. And when he disembarked from his flight, he immediately began scanning the crowd, looking for a woman wearing a green hat and scarf.

Suddenly he saw her, and his heart fell. She was the homeliest person he had ever seen in his life.

He was tempted to hide his carnation and disappear into the crowd. Yet he recalled how caring her e-mail messages had been. After all, he had fallen in love with her, he reasoned. At least he should give her a chance. He walked over to the woman, smiled, and introduced himself.

Immediately the woman said, "What is all this about anyway? I don't know who you are. That woman over there gave me $5 to wear this hat and scarf. Talk to her."

When the man turned around, he saw a beautiful woman sheepishly hanging her head. Slowly she approached him and said, "All my life men have wanted to be with me, to be my friend, because of my looks. I wanted to be sure that you wanted to be with me because of the person that I am inside. I wanted you to love me not just for my outward appearance, but to love me for being me." The two caught each other's gaze and knew that their Internet romance was just the beginning of a lifetime of love.

ADAPTED FROM JAMES S. HEWETT

I love you!

LOVE N CENTS

Look through your scrapbooks and find pictures of you throughout the years. Start with some of the early pictures of you as a baby. Then find some that were taken when you first met her. Make sure to find some current photos, too.

Look for other snapshots that may show you during the holidays, involved in your favorite hobbies, at your office, or on a trip or vacation, etc. Combine the photos in a pleasing arrangement and take them to a copy shop. Ask to have the photos reproduced into a wall or desk calendar for her for the next year. If you have a good "head shot" of yourself, look into making that into a mouse pad for her office or home computer station.

Faith goes up the stairs that love has made and looks out of the windows which hope has opened.

CHARLES SPURGEON

To love is to receive a glimpse of heaven.

KAREN SUNDE

Let your love grow as God wants it to grow; seek goodness in others, love more persons more; love them more impersonally, more unselfishly, without thought of return. The return, never fear, will take care of itself.

HENRY DRUMMOND

We are custodians, keepers of each other's hearts and secrets. We treasure them with tenderness and fidelity. There is always risk when one is dealing with priceless treasures. But we ... prefer to take that risk.

LIONEL A. WHISTON

- Go shopping with her and insist that she try on everything she wants to.
- Rent a billboard and tell everyone that you love her.
- Buy her a gift certificate to a hair or nail salon.
- Compliment her on her new hairdo and manicure.
- Write her a poem and send it with a bouquet of flowers.
- Let her show you how to cook a new recipe.
- Rent a canoe on a moonlit night and sail the seas of love together.
- Remember that romance isn't just a weekend sport.
- Be 30 percent more loving for the next 30 days.
- Remember that staying in love requires consistent action and a conscious decision.
- Go to an adult education class together.
- Create a "romance" category in your budget.
- Give her a $100 gift certificate to her favorite store.
- Show you care with a tender kiss.
- Linger over a kiss to give you a chance to connect on several levels.
- Write notes to her parents to tell them what you've been doing together.
- Visit her relatives with her.
- On Mother's Day or Father's Day send her folks a card, thanking them for their daughter.
- Call her mother just to say hello.
- Ask her mother for the recipe for your wife's favorite dessert.
- Ask God to give you a spirit of love and thankfulness for her family.

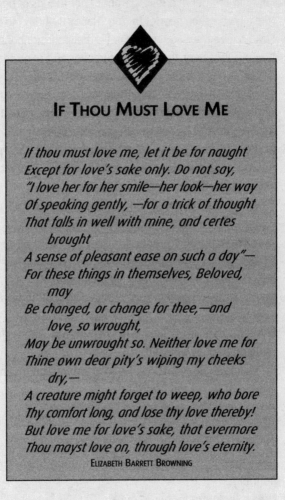

IF THOU MUST LOVE ME

If thou must love me, let it be for naught
Except for love's sake only. Do not say,
"I love her for her smile—her look—her way
Of speaking gently, —for a trick of thought
That falls in well with mine, and certes
    brought
A sense of pleasant ease on such a day"—
For these things in themselves, Beloved,
    may
Be changed, or change for thee,—and
    love, so wrought,
May be unwrought so. Neither love me for
Thine own dear pity's wiping my cheeks
    dry,—
A creature might forget to weep, who bore
Thy comfort long, and lose thy love thereby!
But love me for love's sake, that evermore
Thou mayst love on, through love's eternity.

ELIZABETH BARRETT BROWNING

- Compliment her in public in front of her friends or peers.
- Hire a barbershop quartet to sing "Happy Birthday" to her.
- Flash a love message on a hotel or ballpark signboard.
- If you fight about the same thing over and over again, get to the root of the problem once and for all.
- Go to a drive-in movie together.
- After you've talked on the phone, call her back in a few minutes to tell her how much you miss her.
- On her birthday, make a special display of her baby pictures with the phrase "You must have been a beautiful baby, 'cause baby look at you now!"
- Purposely hold hands when her family is watching.
- Purposely give her a lingering glance in public.
- Back her in her decisions.
- Be honest in your communication.
- Ask, "What can I do to make you happier?"
- Praise her accomplishments to others who come to visit.
- Appreciate her.
- Enter into conversations with her friends rather than hanging back by yourself.
- Be willing to do whatever she asks without grumbling.
- Brag enthusiastically about her.
- Never betray her confidences—keep her secrets.
- Never speak to her with a bitter tone.
- Remember that griping and complaining only leads to resentment—do all things without murmuring or complaining.
- Never apologize for her in public.
- Nurture her in as many ways as possible.

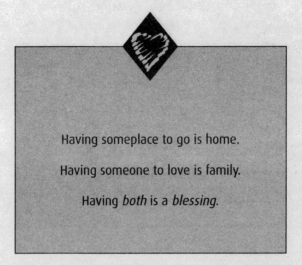

Having someplace to go is home.

Having someone to love is family.

Having *both* is a *blessing*.

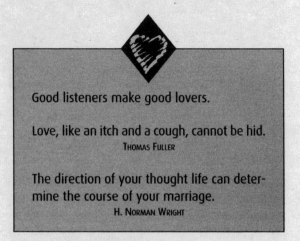

Good listeners make good lovers.

Love, like an itch and a cough, cannot be hid.
THOMAS FULLER

The direction of your thought life can deter-
mine the course of your marriage.
H. NORMAN WRIGHT

LET ME COUNT THE WAYS

Ten reasons you love her even when:

- She stinks up the house with nail polish
- She wants to go shopping again
- She only rents mushy movies
- She spouts off about your friends
- She says "I told you to read the instructions"
- She cooks tuna noodle casserole again
- She has PMS
- She won't go camping and fishing
- She won't wax your truck
- She is without a doubt herself

I have never met a person whose greatest need was anything other than real, unconditional love. You can find it in a simple act of kindness toward someone who needs help. There is no mistaking love. You feel it in your heart. It is the common fiber of life, the flame that heals our soul, energizes our spirit, and supplies passion to our lives. It is our connection to God and to each other.

ELISABETH KIBLER-ROSS

A CHANCE FOR ROMANCE

Childhood field trips to the zoo, museum, or aquarium were always an enjoyable break from routine. But why should kids have all the fun? A day or a weekend trip to a local museum, aquarium, or zoo can be a chance for romance, too. Check out travel and tour books or ask your local library to find some of the best sites in your area.

Pack a picnic lunch to enjoy and be a little silly as you wander through the exhibits—laughter will lighten your heart and get you in a loving mood. Mimic the animals in the zoo. Flap and wiggle like the penguins at the aquarium. Play with the hands-on exhibits in the museum.

To alert your sweetheart to the trip, place a little plastic animal, fish, or dime store gem in a small gift box. Add a note that says: "You're such a great catch (or "find"). How about a trip to the aquarium (or zoo or museum) this weekend?

I love you!

- Have her favorite magazine waiting for her in her chair.
- Suggest she invite her parents over for dinner.
- Hide little gifts around the house for her in places only she will look and find.
- Learn as much as you can about her work.
- Wake her gently with a kiss.
- Give her some private time for hobbies, friends, and time alone.
- Build a snowman together.
- Agree on a place you would like to go together.
- Use the word "ours" instead of "mine" whenever you can.
- Never compare her with old girlfriends, not even in good ways.
- Don't compare her to your mother, even if the comparisons are complimentary.
- Make the date of the month that you met a special day every month thereafter.
- Remind her that she belongs to God.
- Exchange back scratches.
- If she brings work home from the office, ask if you can help.
- Put her phone number in the #1 speed dial position on your work phone.
- Keep a joint journal in which you both can write.
- Be proud of her, and show it, at family reunions.
- Shop with her for costume jewelry.
- Bring home her favorite kind of bagel.

LOVING HER

Use this page to record your feelings about your love for her:

_____

_____

_____

_____

_____

_____

_____

_____

_____

_____

_____

_____

_____

_____

_____

_____

_____

_____

I love you!

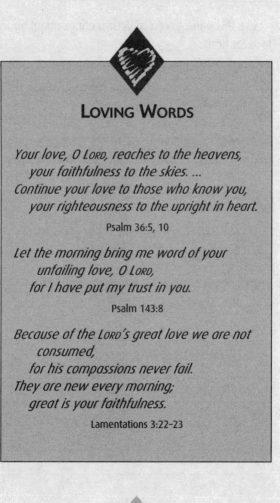

LOVING WORDS

*Your love, O LORD, reaches to the heavens,
 your faithfulness to the skies. ...
Continue your love to those who know you,
 your righteousness to the upright in heart.*

Psalm 36:5, 10

*Let the morning bring me word of your
 unfailing love, O LORD,
 for I have put my trust in you.*

Psalm 143:8

*Because of the LORD's great love we are not
 consumed,
 for his compassions never fail.
They are new every morning;
 great is your faithfulness.*

Lamentations 3:22–23

MORE CARD TRICKS

Make her a personalized greeting card every day this week. Leave it in a different place each time. Here are some quotes you might want to use for the inside greeting or make up some of your own:

The hours I spend with you I look upon as sort of a perfumed garden, a dim twilight, and a fountain singing to it. Other men it is said have seen angels, but I have seen thee and thou art enough.

GEORGE MOORE

I love you,
Not only for what you are,
But for what I am when I am with you.

ROY CROFT

We are each of us angels with only one wing. And we can only fly embracing each other.

LUCIANO DE CRESCENZO

A TIME TO REMIND

Remind her you love her when you ask about her family heritage and try to learn all you can about her roots. Every nationality is rich in customs, folklore, and family traditions.

Ask her about her ancestors. Find out about the family customs and traditions that accompany the holidays. Incorporate as many of her family traditions, customs, foods, and folklore that you can into your relationship. Visit a museum or heritage exhibit to learn more about her background.

All of these pieces of her past have helped make her into the person she is today. Appreciate her for her diversity, for her heritage, for all that she is.

Just as there comes a warm sunbeam into every cottage window, so comes love—born of God's care for every separate need.
NATHANIEL HAWTHORNE

Love is not blind—it sees more, not less. But because it sees more, it is willing to see less.
JULIUS GORDON

Two cannot go in opposite directions if they are in love—love shares a direction of vision.
SMH

Love consists in this: that two solitudes protect and border and greet each other.
RAINER MARIA RILKE

Love is the one business in which it pays to be an absolute spendthrift: Give it away; throw it away; splash it over; empty your pockets; shake the basket; and tomorrow you'll have more than ever.
UNKNOWN

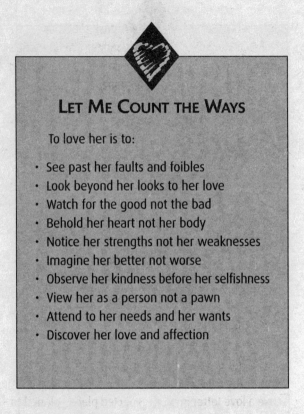

LET ME COUNT THE WAYS

To love her is to:

- See past her faults and foibles
- Look beyond her looks to her love
- Watch for the good not the bad
- Behold her heart not her body
- Notice her strengths not her weaknesses
- Imagine her better not worse
- Observe her kindness before her selfishness
- View her as a person not a pawn
- Attend to her needs and her wants
- Discover her love and affection

- Make your own rituals like giving her a little gift every Wednesday.
- Buy her a bar of soap that smells like lavender.
- Spend a lazy Saturday in a hammock together.
- Offer to take care of the kids (yours or the ones she's responsible for—nieces, nephews, neighbors, etc.) so that she can have some time alone.
- Send her a FedEx letter that says "I love you."
- Have custom stationery, thank you cards, etc. made for her with her monogram.
- Kiss on a chairlift.
- Never watch TV during dinner.
- Help do the grocery shopping.
- Always maintain eye contact when complimenting her.
- Avoid discussions of work, finances, parents, children, or church problems during romantic times.
- Go to the auto parts store and don't charge anything.
- Kiss her hands while she is reading.
- Leave a note asking, "Can we get away this weekend—just you and me?"
- Make a tape-recorded love letter for her.
- Don't neglect your relationship because it's league night at the bowling alley.
- Leave a love letter in an unexpected place—pinned to the inside of her shirt, tucked into her lunch bag, crushed into the toe of a shoe, etc.
- Massage her temples when she has a headache.

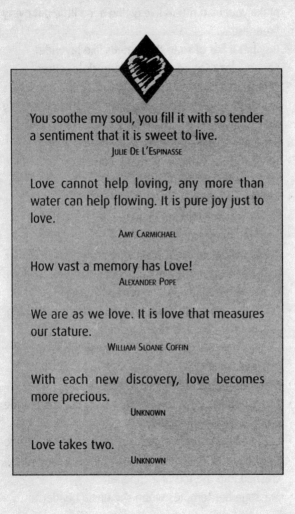

You soothe my soul, you fill it with so tender a sentiment that it is sweet to live.
JULIE DE L'ESPINASSE

Love cannot help loving, any more than water can help flowing. It is pure joy just to love.
AMY CARMICHAEL

How vast a memory has Love!
ALEXANDER POPE

We are as we love. It is love that measures our stature.
WILLIAM SLOANE COFFIN

With each new discovery, love becomes more precious.
UNKNOWN

Love takes two.
UNKNOWN

LOVE N CENTS

See how many ways in one day you can find to surprise her by doing something for her that she always does. Here are some ideas to get your started. Add more ideas of your own and make your own love list.

- Make the bed
- Load the dishwasher
- Buy the groceries
- Put them away
- Shovel the snow from the walk
- Run the errands to the bank and post office
- Set up a babysitter for your next date

- Learn how to say "I love you" in a foreign language and leave it on her voice mail.
- Treat her to a triple scoop cone of her favorite ice cream.
- Budget money regularly for fun.
- Balance the checkbook as soon as the statement arrives.
- Flirt with her at a party.
- Carry a lock of her hair in your wallet.
- Screen her phone calls for her when she is tired; tell folks she'll call them back.
- Make a crazy little gift for her for no reason—a painted rock for a paperweight, etc.
- Serve breakfast to her and her friends before they go off for a day of shopping.
- Hug her from behind and tell her how good she smells.
- Thank her for all the good times.
- Don't put your relationship on hold because it's Super Bowl Sunday.
- Thank her for persevering through the bad times with you.
- Send a bouquet made of little love notes fashioned into flowers.
- Keep love in the pink by giving her a pink rose, a pink outfit, and some pink lemonade.
- Write "I love you" on a cake with icing.
- Chalk a cryptic love message on the driveway.
- Tape a love note to the inside of her closet door.
- During a winter walk, surprise her with a thermos of hot cocoa.
- Make her a custom gingerbread lady for Christmas.

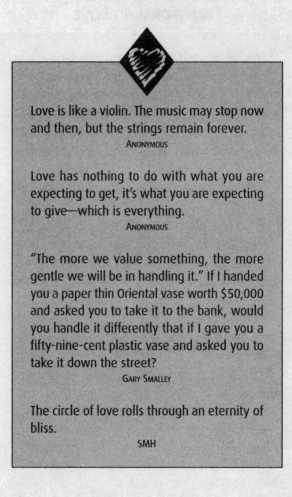

Love is like a violin. The music may stop now and then, but the strings remain forever.
ANONYMOUS

Love has nothing to do with what you are expecting to get, it's what you are expecting to give—which is everything.
ANONYMOUS

"The more we value something, the more gentle we will be in handling it." If I handed you a paper thin Oriental vase worth $50,000 and asked you to take it to the bank, would you handle it differently that if I gave you a fifty-nine-cent plastic vase and asked you to take it down the street?
GARY SMALLEY

The circle of love rolls through an eternity of bliss.
SMH

TRANSFORMING LOVE

Jean was a gray-haired woman who sang alto at church choir practice. Quiet and unassuming, she tended to blend into the background. She came and went, sang and left. I guess I never truly saw Jean until the day I met her husband, Al, as he picked her up from choir. From that moment, my perception of Jean was forever altered.

"Isn't she something?" Al said, nudging me with an elbow as he smiled and winked at his bride of thirty years. "That woman brings me so much joy."

Pale, quiet Jean did something I would never have expected. She blushed. Al went on applauding her attributes, building her up with his words. And she began to blossom. Right there before my eyes.

A prolific poet, Al asked if he could quote me a poem about his wife, and I said, "Of course! You must!"

"Oh, Al ...," she muttered, embarrassed yet pleased.

I don't remember the words of his poem, but the beauty I saw unfold from deep within Jean I shall never forget. It changed the lowly alto into one of the most beautiful women I've ever seen.

Transforming love. The kind that lasts despite time and age, sagging lips and flabby hips. The kind that sticks around when we're not as wonderful as we could be or should be.

The kind of love that still softly glows, though her lover and his poems have since been silenced by the ravages of Alzheimer's disease. In the three short years since I'd seen them last, Jean's vibrant husband had disappeared, leaving an empty shell. My eyes filled with tears as I expressed my sympathy and how hard it must be.

"It's not hard to love," Jean told me, bending down to tuck in a lap quilt around the emaciated legs of her beloved Al. She kissed him softly on the cheek. "Not when you've been loved like I've been loved."

JOANNA WEAVER

I love you!

A TIME TO REMIND

Remind her you love her when she sees that she has inspired you to greatness.

Emulate her caring concern for others by willingly reaching out to help a neighbor or co-worker in distress.

Follow her example of trustworthiness by following through on your promises, calling when you'll be late and letting her know where you'll be if you're not home.

Use her as a role model to strive for excellence in your work, openness in your relationships, and determination in your attempts to solve interpersonal problems.

Let her life be your example of how to have a closer walk with God, a deeper sense of his presence, and a renewed commitment to sharing your witness.

Celebrate her input in your life with a letter of thanks detailing all of the ways her life has been a positive example for you.

MR. FIX IT

To bring a smile to the lady of your life, use your tools and put together a "working man's picnic." Shake out your drop cloth and give it a good washing. Pop your tools out of your toolbox and clean the box up until it sparkles like new. Line the inside of it with bubble wrap secured with a few pieces of duct tape. Clean out your tool belt, too, or buy a new one. The drop cloth, tool belt and tool box are essential to this picnic.

Put together the foods you'd like to take on your picnic. If you like to cook, make one of your favorite recipes. If you prefer sandwiches, build the best ones you can. Or, if you'd prefer to the let the Colonel do your cooking, make a stop at a fried chicken stand and purchase all of the pieces necessary for a picnic.

Fill your toolbox with the prepared foods and paper plates. Hang silverware, napkins, cups, and a 20 ounce bottle of soda on your tool belt. Put the tool box, tool belt, and drop cloth in the back of the car, put on your best cap, and go pick up your lady. Find a shady spot out of the main traffic lanes in the home improvement store parking lot and spread out your drop cloth. Surprise your lady with your "working man's picnic" in a toolbox as you laugh together and enjoy the day.

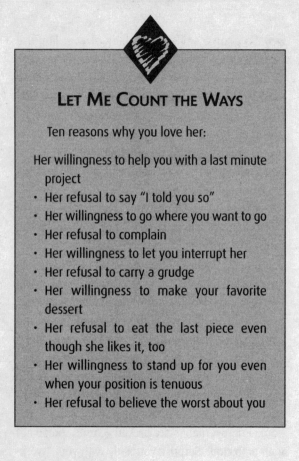

LET ME COUNT THE WAYS

Ten reasons why you love her:

Her willingness to help you with a last minute project
- Her refusal to say "I told you so"
- Her willingness to go where you want to go
- Her refusal to complain
- Her willingness to let you interrupt her
- Her refusal to carry a grudge
- Her willingness to make your favorite dessert
- Her refusal to eat the last piece even though she likes it, too
- Her willingness to stand up for you even when your position is tenuous
- Her refusal to believe the worst about you

A DAY AWAY

Surprise her with a day away. Call in to work and take the day off. Turn your pager and cell phone off. Don't consult the clock—just enjoy the day and do what you want to do when you want to do it. It doesn't matter if the day is rainy or bright sunshine—enjoy the day away with each other.

Climb into the car and drive to her favorite park or nature spot. Go to the mall and wander through her favorite stores. Take a cab to a museum or art gallery. Go to a matinee or take in a "spot of tea" at a 5-star hotel. Have a leisurely lunch somewhere you've always wanted to go.

Window shop in some expensive downtown stores. Actually wander into a jewelry store and try on a few rings and bracelets. Laugh a lot. Listen a lot. Smile even more.

And when the day is done, linger on the porch and watch the stars come out. She's worth it.

I love you!

The loving are the daring.
BAYARD TAYLOR

Love is a force more formidable than any other. It is invisible—it cannot be seen or measured, yet it is powerful enough to transform you in a moment, and offer you more joy that any material possession could.
BARBARA DE ANGELIS

There is often more pleasure in loving another than in being the object of another's love.
ANONYMOUS

Love is the beauty of a soul.
ST. AUGUSTINE

A CHANCE FOR ROMANCE

When she's sick be a doctor of love:

Put together a "hope you feel better" kit. Fill it with tissues, soup mix, cold tablets, aspirin, throat lozenges, a candy or two—Hershey's Kisses® are nice. Include a funny video and some magazines. An inspirational book or favorite novel for reading would be good choices, too.

Offer to run any errands for her that she needs to get done. Call her office to report her as sick. Make sure the cookie jar is filled with her favorite cookies, and that she has snacks whenever she wants them.

Tuck her into bed and let her feel pampered even though she's sick. She'll recover quicker and will love you for your good bedside manner. When she recovers, she'll tell her friends, too, so be prepared to share with other guys your tips for treating the sick.

I love you!

- Learn to sew on your own buttons.
- Believe her when she says she heard a strange noise in the house.
- Don't rearrange the contents of the kitchen cupboards to make them "more efficient."
- Don't eat all the walnuts, coconut, hot fudge, or other food items without letting her know—she might have had plans for them.
- Realize that six tickets to the tractor pull—for you, her, and your four buddies from the garage—may not be her first choice for a fun night out.
- Don't put your relationship on hold because deer season started.
- After she's been away, meet her at the airport in your Sunday best. Have her favorite music playing in the house when she returns.
- Make her late for breakfast by telling her how much you love her.
- Plant flowers outside a window so that she'll see them every morning.
- Be patient with each other.
- Learn to iron your own shirts.
- Share a juicy red apple.
- Give her a Saturday off from chores.
- Listen 20 percent more than you talk.
- Do the pots and pans after a big dinner.
- Share your feelings more than you do facts.

- When it isn't even her birthday, arrange a surprise party with all of her friends.
- Have a five-course meal sent to her at work for lunch.
- Have a photo calendar made with all of her favorite photos.
- Send her a different CD of love songs each day for a week.
- Make goofy pictures at a "four-for-a-dollar" photo machine and have them framed.
- Send her a reminder card that expresses your undying love and affection.
- Take a hayride on an autumn afternoon.
- Go Christmas shopping together in the middle of July.
- Play hide and seek in the dark.
- Keep her favorite flavor of ice cream in the freezer at all times.
- Remember that chocolate is always the right choice when saying I love you.
- Try expressing your love through the delivery of a single rose in a crystal bud vase.
- Tell her you love her, without saying a word.
- Love her by letting her sit in your arms without saying much of anything.
- Send her a giant teddy bear to hug when you aren't there.
- Sit quietly by the fire and tell her all the things you adore about her.
- Take her to the edge of town late at night to look for shooting stars together.
- Send her a heart cut out of construction paper with your names written on it in crayon.

LOVING WORDS

As God's chosen people, holy and dearly loved, clothe yourselves with compassion, kindness, humility, gentleness and patience. ... Over all these virtues put on love, which binds them all together in perfect unity.

Colossians 3:12, 14

God created us to connect to each other. He made us with the need for other people ... Communion is what happens whenever spirits are shared and cups are filled with love. It's what happens whenever human beings draw near to each other and to God, managing somehow to emerge from their separateness and partake of the shared life God intended.

EMILIE BARNES

Jesus prayed, "I pray also for those who will believe in me through [my disciples'] message, that all of them may be one, Father, just as you are in me and I am in you."

John 17:20–21

LOVING HER

Use this page to record your feelings about your love for her:

_____

_____

_____

_____

_____

_____

_____

_____

_____

_____

_____

_____

_____

_____

I love you!

_____

_____

_____

GREAT DATES

Couples who are best friends know how to put the sparkle back in their love life by having great dates. Here are a few suggestions of some dates you could try.

A Photo Date: Purchase a disposable camera. Go to your favorite haunts and start snapping away. Ask a bystander to take your picture together. Keep snapping until all of the shots are used. Drop the camera at a one-hour developing place and talk over coffee until the pictures are ready.

Too-Tired Date: Put on your most comfy loungewear. Order takeout food, turn on the answering machine, and just relax in front of a favorite video or snuggled together on the couch with copies of your favorite books.

Gourmet Cooking Date: Plan the menu, do the grocery shopping together at an upscale market, and cook your dinner together! Experiment with new ideas and menu items. Bon appetit!

DAVID & CLAUDIA ARP

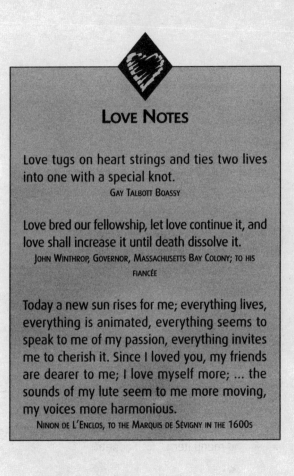

LOVE NOTES

Love tugs on heart strings and ties two lives into one with a special knot.

GAY TALBOTT BOASSY

Love bred our fellowship, let love continue it, and love shall increase it until death dissolve it.

JOHN WINTHROP, GOVERNOR, MASSACHUSETTS BAY COLONY; TO HIS FIANCÉE

Today a new sun rises for me; everything lives, everything is animated, everything seems to speak to me of my passion, everything invites me to cherish it. Since I loved you, my friends are dearer to me; I love myself more; ... the sounds of my lute seem to me more moving, my voices more harmonious.

NINON DE L'ENCLOS, TO THE MARQUIS DE SÉVIGNY IN THE 1600s

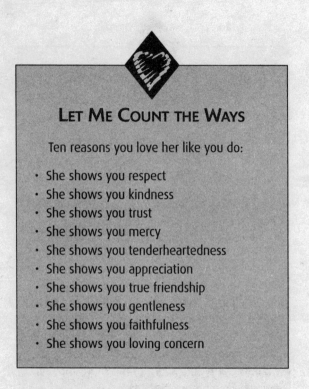

LET ME COUNT THE WAYS

Ten reasons you love her like you do:

- She shows you respect
- She shows you kindness
- She shows you trust
- She shows you mercy
- She shows you tenderheartedness
- She shows you appreciation
- She shows you true friendship
- She shows you gentleness
- She shows you faithfulness
- She shows you loving concern

BECAUSE

I love you because you always tell me
  to drive carefully, wear a coat,
  get some rest, and stop worrying.
Why should I worry?
I have you.

When I'm late getting home,
  you're worried and pacing the floor,
  looking for me or calling the neighbors.
Your love makes me feel safe, cared for.

I love you because you take me seriously—
  you're concerned that I'm working too hard,
  worrying too much,
  aren't appreciated enough, or don't relax
    enough.
When you're so concerned about me,
I don't have to be.

DIANNA BOOHER

- Call her every day when you're on a business trip even if you have to pay for the call yourself.
- Hold on a little longer with your hugs.
- Linger a little longer with your kisses.
- Make her a wreath for her office door out of Hershey's Kisses®.
- Purchase a dated Christmas tree ornament for your anniversary.
- Help her find ways to simplify her life.
- Learn to Rollerblade together.
- Buy her a pint of gourmet ice cream.
- Forgive any grudges you may be carrying.
- Put up a bird feeder where she will be able to see it and reach it.
- Surprise her with a candlelight dinner.
- Work to lose the weight you gained last year so that you will feel better when you're with her.
- Help her organize her old photos.
- Give her the gift of time by doing some of her chores for her or making supper unexpectedly.
- Give her a coupon for a soft ice cream cone at the Dairy Queen®—to be redeemed anytime she wants it.
- Leave a love note on the refrigerator door with magnetic letters.
- Slip a foil wrapped chocolate heart into her purse with a note attached that reads: "You've stolen my heart."
- Give her a coupon for breakfast in bed that can be redeemed this month.
- Put together a picnic in the middle of winter.
- Treat her as if she were a princess.

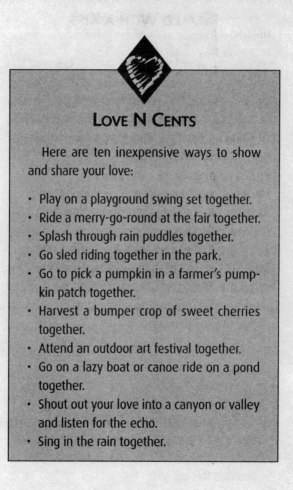

LOVE N CENTS

Here are ten inexpensive ways to show and share your love:

- Play on a playground swing set together.
- Ride a merry-go-round at the fair together.
- Splash through rain puddles together.
- Go sled riding together in the park.
- Go to pick a pumpkin in a farmer's pumpkin patch together.
- Harvest a bumper crop of sweet cherries together.
- Attend an outdoor art festival together.
- Go on a lazy boat or canoe ride on a pond together.
- Shout out your love into a canyon or valley and listen for the echo.
- Sing in the rain together.

SEALED WITH A KISS

Though fairy tales tell of princes claiming the love of princesses with kiss-filled courtships, Gordon and Maggie's relationship was different. In the past, Gordon had stolen kisses from girlfriends. But when Gordon took Maggie home from their first date and bent to kiss her good night, Maggie ducked her head. Gordon's lips only grazed her forehead.

In a shy, quiet voice Maggie apologized for taking Gordon so by surprise. Then she told Gordon of her childhood vow to never kiss anyone until she kissed her husband on her wedding day. Gordon said good night to Maggie, but then went home and told his roommate about this unusual girl and her unusual ways. Her commitment to purity strengthened his resolve to see her again.

The months flew by filled with picnics, long walks, bike rides, and dinners shared with friends. Slowly they realized that the flower of love was blossoming. They opened their lives to each other, sharing their dreams and touching each other's hearts. But at the close of every date, Gordon respected Maggie's wishes, leaving her on her doorstep with a hug or a tightly clasped hand.

That November they were engaged; and on the first day of summer the pastor pronounced them man and wife. As Gordon lifted Maggie's veil to give her their first kiss, both he and she stood before God knowing that they were pure, holy and blameless. With giggling abandon, they sealed their marriage vows with love's first kiss—everything they had waited for and more.

Now, twenty-five years later, Gordon and Maggie still enjoy holding hands, stealing a kiss in the middle of the mall, sharing a glance across the kitchen table. Waiting for God's best has meant a life of laughter, sharing, growing, and loving. What more could any couple want?

SARAH HUPP

I love you!

MR. FIX IT

Bring a smile to your lady's face with a visit from Duct Tape Man! If you've had a silly quarrel, you need to patch things up. A little duct tape may just do the trick.

Show up at her workplace, or while she's getting her hair done, or shopping at the grocery store with several rolls of duct tape lining your arms. If you're able, wrap up as much of yourself as you can in duct tape, making sure that one piece is emblazoned with the name "Duct Tape Man" and is worn on a highly visible place like your chest or cap.

Apologize for the quarrel and offer to patch things up with your duct tape. If she's had some time to cool off from the quarrel, she'll probably giggle and hug you right there in the middle of your rolls of tape.

In the future, you might want to keep a roll of duct tape handy for patching up other things that might come up, too.

- Keep a photo at work of the woman you love. If possible, keep it where you will see it several times a day.
- Send her a love letter every day the week before your anniversary.
- Plant a rosebush, a tree, or some other long-lived garden plant that symbolizes your long-lasting commitment to each other.
- Consider buying her a sewing machine before you buy a motorcycle.
- Write a letter to her telling her why you would want to meet her and get to know her all over again.
- Realize that she may not see the gift of a work bench for the garage as an appropriate anniversary present.
- Eat, at least once, any new recipe she tries.
- Let her use the barbeque grill.
- Don't criticize her barbeque skills even if she burns the burgers.
- Never, never, never take her for granted.
- Buy a bouquet of roses for her "just because."
- Enjoy her company.
- Make reservations at that bed and breakfast she's been telling you about.
- Believe her when she says you're terrific.
- Make a list of all the wonderful things that have happened in your life since you've known her.
- Take her for a ride in a hot air balloon.
- Clean out your closet before she asks you to.
- Ask if you can help her organize her CDs and videos.
- Set aside one evening a month for a game night. Play what she wants to play.

A TIME TO REMIND

Take time to remind her how much you love her by arranging a formal "Dinner in the Park" date. Both of you dress up in your best evening wear—black tie and formal evening gown. Grab a picnic basket and head for a quiet spot in a city park or on a bluff overlooking the lights of the city. Don't bother with folding chairs. A good-sized blanket spread on the ground will protect your clothing and give you a comfortable place for your alfresco dinner.

Bring along a battery operated cassette or CD player and play quiet mood music as you enjoy your night under the stars. Better yet, consult your local paper to see if an outdoor concert may be scheduled nearby and include that in your "Dinner in the Park" date. End the evening by making a wish together on a star for many more wonderful evenings to come.

Men want to be a woman's first love. That is their clumsy vanity. Women have a more subtle instinct about things. They like to be a man's last romance.

ANONYMOUS

Don't bypass the potential for meaningful relationships just because of differences. Explore them. Embrace them. Love them.

LUCI SWINDOLL

Love warms all who come under its power and lightens all hearts who yield to its influence.

SMH

There is no surprise more magical than the surprise of being loved. It is God's finger on man's shoulder.

CHARLES MORGAN

Love can hope where reason would despair.

BARON GEORGE LYTTELTON

Soon after our last child left home for college, my husband was resting next to me on the couch with his head in my lap. I carefully removed his glasses. "You know, honey," I said sweetly, "without your glasses you look like the same handsome young man I married."

"Honey," he replied with a grin, "without my glasses, you still look pretty good too!"

VALERIE L. RUNYAN

On her golden wedding anniversary, my grandmother revealed the secret of her long and happy marriage. "On my wedding day, I decided to choose ten of my husband's faults which, for the sake of our marriage, I would overlook," she explained.

A guest asked her to name some of the faults. "To tell the truth," she replied, "I never did get around to listing them. But whenever my husband did something that made me hopping mad, I would say to myself, ' Lucky for him that's one of the ten.'"

RODERICK MCFARLANE

Real love is a slow growth coming from unity of life and purpose. Love is a product. It is a thing to be created by mutual service and sacrifice.

ELTON TRUEBLOOD

REAL LOVE IS ...

- Watching that sappy movie with her when your favorite team is playing on TV
- Holding her when she's sick in bed and probably contagious
- Bringing home a bucket of chicken so she won't have to cook.
- Always being there for her, through the good times and the bad.

LOVE AND LAUGHTER

Make this a loving, laughter-filled day for her. Here are some suggestions to get you started:

Send her a funny e-mail.

Recall a time when something embarrassing happened. Can you laugh about it now with her?

Pop a humor cassette or CD in her car stereo system so that she will have something to laugh about on her way to work.

Recall a time when you were surprised by happiness or laughter. Share a story about that time with her.

Leave a joke or funny comic strip on the mirror.

Smile a goofy smile and make her laugh.

Talk about the favorite places you have lived or visited that really made you smile.

Look for ways to take yourself less seriously. Play with little children's toys at an adult dinner party, have a water balloon fight, challenge each other to design a wacky hat and wear it out to dinner!

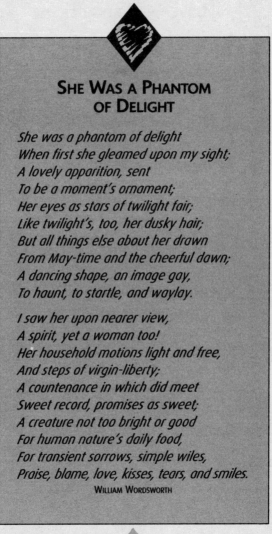

SHE WAS A PHANTOM OF DELIGHT

She was a phantom of delight
When first she gleamed upon my sight;
A lovely apparition, sent
To be a moment's ornament;
Her eyes as stars of twilight fair;
Like twilight's, too, her dusky hair;
But all things else about her drawn
From May-time and the cheerful dawn;
A dancing shape, an image gay,
To haunt, to startle, and waylay.

I saw her upon nearer view,
A spirit, yet a woman too!
Her household motions light and free,
And steps of virgin-liberty;
A countenance in which did meet
Sweet record, promises as sweet;
A creature not too bright or good
For human nature's daily food,
For transient sorrows, simple wiles,
Praise, blame, love, kisses, tears, and smiles.

WILLIAM WORDSWORTH

THE LANGUAGE OF LOVE

I've learned the Lord's language of love. When I tell Jesus that I love him, it has nothing to do with romance. But passion? Yes! My love for Jesus is not a syrupy sentiment, but it is definitely zealous and fervent, spirited and intense. When I praise him, I want the melody to come right from my heart.

And this is the way we are to love our brothers and sisters. Throw your caution to the wind and invite the Spirit of God to fill your heart with the warmth and passion of praise. And love others with the same warmth and affection you reserve for him.

JONI EARECKSON TADA

How can you share this new insight with the one you love? Does she know the Lord's language of love?

- Keep a definition of love in the calendar you carry around to help keep your life in a loving perspective.
- Don't let irritations make you angry—let a "soft answer" and a smile be your response.
- Let her invite her friends over for a home sales party (Tupperware®, Mary Kay®, or Pampered Chef®) and offer to serve snacks and clean up.
- Give hugs when the day has been especially tough for her—and when it has been especially easy, too!
- Rent a convertible and take a leisurely drive until the stars come out.
- Rock in a double rocker on the screened porch, holding hands.
- Do something together that goes beyond obligation.
- Secretly pass a love note to her during a serious budget meeting at church.
- While riding in an elevator, tell her she looks wonderful.
- Help her with a crossword puzzle.
- Issue her a coupon entitling her to one hour of cuddling in a location of her choice.
- Don't let one day go by without telling her how beautiful she is.
- Be aware of current events and concerned enough to talk about these things with her.
- Keep yourself healthy.
- Take one day at a time.
- Don't be afraid of the dust rag or polishing cloth—you can conquer those tools, too.

LOVING WORDS

Do not forget to do good and to share with others, for with such sacrifices God is pleased.

Hebrews 13:16

Carry each other's burdens, and in this way you will fulfill the law of Christ.

Galatians 6:2

Jesus said, "Love the Lord your God with all your heart and with all your soul and with all your mind and with all your strength. ... Love your neighbor as yourself. There is no commandment greater than these."

Mark 12:30-31

A generous man will prosper; he who refreshes others will himself be refreshed.

Proverbs 11:25

THE MYSTERY OF LOVE

Keeping a healthy, growing relationship requires friendship, fun, and romance. And there's nothing like a mystery date to encourage all of these facets of love to flower and grow.

Start now to plan your mystery date. Keep the destination and arrangements secret for as long as possible. Allow guessing, but don't reveal too much with your answers. After all, this date is a mystery! You might even want to blindfold your sweetheart until you've reached your final destination and have her try to guess where you're going by the sounds and smells along the way.

The date might include a concert, a favorite or new restaurant, or even a surprise getaway. But don't over-schedule your date. Be sure to include some time for communicating and reviving the spark that brought you two together in the first place.

I love you!

A TIME TO REMIND

Take time to remind her you love her when you look into the future with her. No one can predict what will happen to any of us over the next decade. So, why not make a time capsule that incorporates some of the essences of who you two are right now in this place in your relationship. Record your values, your church, your history together, and how you met. Include recent photos of yourselves and a description of your most treasured possession. Write down a testimony of your personal faith, too. Then list some goals and dreams and plans that the two of you share.

Bury your time capsule in a corner of the backyard, behind a loose brick in the basement, underneath a pile of junk in the attic, or any other place where it will remain undisturbed for some time. Then give each other a kiss, knowing that you've left your mark of love on the world.

LOVING THE ABCs

Let the alphabet help you find ways to tell her you love her ...

Using her name as a starting point, create an acrostic that illustrates why you love her. Example: For a girl named "Joan" you might choose "J" oyful; "O" ptimistic; "A" ttractive; "N" ice.

Then use the alphabet and come up with as many of her wonderful qualities that you can think of to go with each letter of the alphabet. Here are a few to get you started:

A = amazing, attitude, athletic, attractive
B = believable, best, beautiful, brave
C = charming, caring, compassionate, considerate
D = daring, diligent, dedicated, decisive

LET ME COUNT THE WAYS

Ten reasons why you love her:

- Her dependability
- Her honesty
- Her congeniality
- Her loving glances
- Her secret graces
- Her unsung deeds
- Her consistency
- Her values
- Her willingness to help
- Her need to be needed

MR. FIX IT

If you are like lots of men, you probably have more than one baseball cap. But you probably only wear one special cap all of the time. Here's your chance to recycle those extra caps and show your sweetheart that you love her, too.

Gather your old caps together. The ones with the clip adjustable backs will work best for this project. Clip caps together until you have a long line of caps. Then clip the last cap in the line onto the first cap. You now should have a circle of caps.

Slide this circle of caps onto your bare feet. Take a photo of your feet wearing the ring of caps. Get it developed and blown up to a 5 x 7 size. Sign the photo, "I'm head over heels for you!" and frame it for a "just because" present.

And now that you've pulled all those caps together, why not give them away to a second hand store so that someone else can actually wear them!

I love you!

JUST FOR FUN

To keep the mystery and interest alive in your relationship, why not try one or two of these dating ideas just for fun!

Go out for a drive on the back roads. See if you can get lost and then find your way home again. If you know the area too well, try driving in one direction for three minutes and then change direction at the next crossroads and drive for another three minutes. Continue this process for an hour. You'll probably see some territory you've never seen before. Stop along the way and grab a snack at a new restaurant. The only problem is, if you like the restaurant, you may never be able to find it again!

Send her a mysterious "treasure map" to lead her to a secret rendezvous. Have a meal planned and something to do, too, like a game of mini golf, a concert, or a stroll by a stream when she finally finds you.

Go sailing in a small sailboat on a nearby lake. Rent a wave runner if you prefer something noisier and faster, or try a small boat with an outboard motor. Find a secluded spot along shore and enjoy some time just sitting and watching the water.

LOVE N CENTS

Here are ten inexpensive ways to show and share your love:

- Go for a lazy bike ride through a park or wooded glen.
- Buy a disposable camera and take photos of each other as you ride.
- Develop the photos and have one made into a jigsaw puzzle.
- Take time to put the puzzle together.
- Reward each other for a job well done with a double-dip ice cream cone.
- Give her an Eskimo kiss (rub noses).
- Buy her favorite kind of chewing gum.
- Learn to say "I love you" in at least five different languages.
- Read and discuss a book together.
- Nibble on her ear.

Do's and Don'ts

Ten do's and don'ts to keep your love alive:

- Don't tattoo her name on your arm in a big heart.
- Do engrave her name on your heart.
- Don't send a guy in a gorilla suit to proclaim your love during her home Bible study.
- Do hide a bookmark in her Bible that tells her how much you love her.
- Don't toast your love with a glass of prune juice.
- Do toast your love with her favorite sparkling beverage.
- Don't call her an old girlfriend's nickname.
- Do give her a special name that only you two know.

A LOVE THAT TRIUMPHED

Elizabeth Barrett spent most of her life as a secluded invalid under the domination of her wealthy, widower father. Although she remained a recluse, Elizabeth began submitting her poetry to various publications, which brought her to the attention of Robert Browning, whose poetry she also enjoyed.

The two authors began a long correspondence with each other, and, eventually Browning received permission to visit Elizabeth at her home in London. Their romance flourished the following year, giving the confined invalid new strength and encouragement. Browning finally persuaded Elizabeth to become his wife, and she did so in secret, without her father's consent. One week later, she left her home forever, fleeing with her husband to Italy where they had a happy and contented life with each other.

These two passionate, eloquent people left the world a wealth of moving, ardent verses in poetry and letters to each other. Mrs. Browning's "Sonnets from the Portuguese" are an especially touching tribute to her lover and a timeless expression of love for all.

- Learn to sing a French love song.
- Touch each other often by giving hugs every chance you get.
- Unconditionally accept each other.
- Agree to never tickle her super sensitive feet.
- Stare deeply into her eyes and see your love reflected back to you.
- Give her the freedom to be different.
- Recognize your need for growth and change.
- Compromise cheerfully when necessary.
- Let her operate in her areas of strength.
- Learn from her.
- Always do for her what you would want her to do for you.
- Send her a romantic e-mail message several times a week.
- Call if you're running late.
- Learn to tap out "I love you" in Morse code.
- Bake her a cake in the shape of a heart or a flower.
- Buy her a watch with your photo inserted on the face.
- Keep extra batteries around for her electronic gadgets and gizmos.
- Spray your after shave in her car.
- Take her off her pedestal and place her by your side.
- Be a mentor to a young man and show him how he should treat a lady by the way you treat yours!
- Light a fire in the fireplace and read love poems to her.
- Carry all of her things (packages, purse, briefcase, diaper bag, etc.) and let her walk empty-handed.

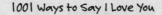

THINK ABOUT THIS

In one sense, we have so much in common it is remarkable we don't understand each other better. We are of the same flesh. We are of the same species. We are genetically and biologically connected. Every woman receives half her DNA from a man. Every man receives half his DNA from a woman.

Yet, in another sense, men and women are as different as night from day—as beauty from the beast, as sandpaper from silk, as rose from thorn—exactly the way God intended.

PATRICK M. MORLEY

We decided early to establish a regularly scheduled "date night"! Just the two of us, alone. To laugh, to lift our spirits, to love. It puts the two of us more at ease with each other during the remainder of the week.

Because we are changing persons in a changing world, we are constantly becoming reacquainted with each other. As a result, we have grown together—not apart—as the years have passed. How blessed are those who experience the priceless discovery of love!

ROBERT & ARVELLA SCHULLER

A TIME TO REMIND

Take time to remind her you love her when you bring a carryout dinner home in an unusual way. It may take a little planning, but the extra effort will be worth it.

Purchase boxes or tins in graduated sizes. Line each box or tin with a zippered storage bag. Order her favorite Chinese, Thai, Italian, or Greek meal. Place each dinner item in a separate container. Stack the containers in order of size with the largest one on the bottom. Tie them all together with a colorful, wide ribbon and a big floppy bow.

Deliver the stacked containers with a folded towel on your arm and a low bow. The twinkle in her eye and the smile on her face will make the meal taste even better than it looks.

Man loves with his eyes and a woman with her ears.

IRISH SAYING

Love gives itself; it is not bought.
Nothing can melt the coldest heart, save the heat of love's eternal flame.

R.R. WASHINGTON

Love grows of its own free will; it cannot be commanded.

UNKNOWN

LET ME COUNT THE WAYS

Come up with an alphabetical list for loving her:

Always beautiful
Completely desirable
Exceptionally friendly
Great hearted
Infectiously joyful
Kind and loving
Magnanimous and nice
Overtly persistent
Quite responsible
Super trusting
Undeniably vulnerable
Wonderful and zany

- Give your beloved a Christmas ornament each year that highlights a special memory.
- Walk barefoot in the ocean together.
- Make a donation to a homeless shelter or crisis pregnancy center in her honor.
- Remind yourself every day how blessed you are to have her in your life.
- Don't take what she does for you and others for granted.
- Look for opportunities to forgive, rather than condemn.
- Let something she did wrong go without comment.
- Place a single red rose in her briefcase.
- When apart, think about each other for one minute at a pre-determined time.
- Believe that the best is yet to come.
- Learn the sign language signal for "I love you."
- Give away that ugly moose head that has been molting over your mantle for years.
- Let her keep her aunt's old Victorian lamp on the desk even though it doesn't work.
- Don't try to fix her aunt's old Victorian lamp unless she asks you to.
- Buy tickets to go see her favorite opera.
- Go with her to see her favorite opera.
- Buy her her favorite snacks to eat during a movie or concert.
- Find out where the symphony plays its outdoor summer concerts and take her unexpectedly.
- Buy a box of sparklers and set them off on her birthday.
- Take out an ad in the local paper to tell everyone how wonderful she is.

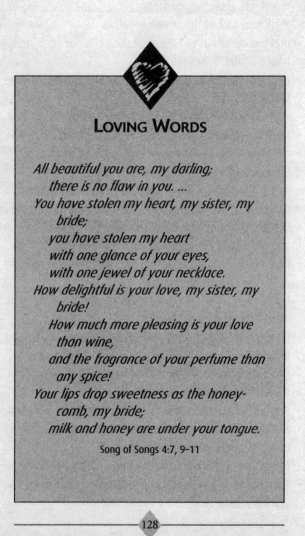

LOVING WORDS

All beautiful you are, my darling;
there is no flaw in you. ...
You have stolen my heart, my sister, my
bride;
you have stolen my heart
with one glance of your eyes,
with one jewel of your necklace.
How delightful is your love, my sister, my
bride!
How much more pleasing is your love
than wine,
and the fragrance of your perfume than
any spice!
Your lips drop sweetness as the honey-
comb, my bride;
milk and honey are under your tongue.

Song of Songs 4:7, 9–11

A Time to Remind

Take the time to remind him you love him when you ...

- Bake his favorite cake.
- Take him a cold drink while he's mowing the grass.
- Help him on his next car repair project.
- Make him his favorite meal, even if it's only hot dogs and beans!
- Read and learn about his favorite hobby or sport.
- Write him a love letter and send it to his work address.
- Get his car washed, waxed, and filled with gas.
- Listen to him share about his day without interrupting.
- Fill the cookie jar with his favorite cookies.
- Hide a note of encouragement in his briefcase.

- Be yourself.
- Go for long walks together.
- Be patient with each other.
- Write "I Love You" on the steamy mirror when he's in the shower.
- Say you are sorry.
- Buy yourself something sexy that he will enjoy, too.
- Be nice to his mother.
- Let him have "the guys" over.
- Give him a Saturday off.
- Share a juicy orange.
- Hang his picture in your office.
- Clean out his car without publicizing it.
- Cuddle together in front of the fireplace, not the TV.
- Listen.
- Leave him a sexy message on his voice mail at work.
- Buy him his favorite candy.
- Watch two hours of football without complaint.
- Send him a funny fax.
- Share his dreams.
- Tell him you're glad you married him.
- Never, never nag (or if you must, only occassionally!).
- Celebrate his differences.
- Surprise him with a kiss in public.
- Curb your desire to mold him, change him, or remake him.
- Change one of your bad habits.

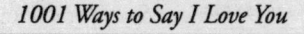

Let Me Count the Ways

Ten reasons why you love him:

1. His laugh
2. His eyes
3. His caring heart
4. His smile
5. His strong arms
6. His gentle hands
7. His sense of humor
8. His voice
9. His protective nature
10. His love for you

Jim and Patty

He wanted to make it her dream come true. Jim and Patty had been married in a simple ceremony with four friends looking on. Patty had worn a borrowed wedding gown. There hadn't been enough money for a reception, so Jim had dreamed of making their twenty-fifth anniversary the wedding they never had. But Lou Gehrig's disease entered the picture, and now Jim had less than a year to live.

Without Patty's knowledge, Jim began piecing together his anniversary surprise. For a person in perfect health, a wedding is a huge project. But for Jim's trembling hands and increasing paralysis, the project was a near impossibility. Yet Jim refused to give in.

When Jim and his daughters couldn't find bridesmaids dresses they liked, he traded a used copier for a sewing machine and made the off-the-shoulder burgundy satin dresses himself, even though he'd never sewn a seam in his life.

Jim took care of the flowers, music, cake, and photographer. No detail was left undone. Jim and his girls even shopped for Patty's wedding dress, though he was disappointed that he no longer had the strength to make her dress, too. And then Jim told Patty about the plan.

"I can't guarantee I will be around next year," Jim said. "So let me marry you properly now." Patty was stunned when she heard about all that Jim and the girls had put together. With tears and smiles, she agreed to marry Jim once again.

The following evening Jim and Patty Porter stood in the flickering candlelight in a decorated chapel not far from their home. Friends and family filled the pews and cried with bittersweet joy as Jim and Patty again exchanged the holy vows they had spoken so many years before. Twenty-four years of Jim's love was finally wrapped up in a memory that would last Patty a lifetime. Could there be a more wonderful way to say, "I love you"?

JOANNA WEAVER

- Let him wear his favorite hat—even if it's grungy.
- Forgive him.
- Listen to his favorite kind of music without complaint.
- Give hugs and kisses often.
- Eat a snack together and enjoy the quiet time.
- Leave a loving message on a sticky note on his car's rearview mirror.
- Watch a romantic movie.
- Keep a picture of the two of you in plain sight.
- Always kiss goodbye.
- Tuck a love note in or on his lunch bag.
- Send your sweetie a humorous or romantic card every day for a week.
- Take time to laugh together.
- Give him a back rub.
- Play a game together.
- Become his best friend.
- Light a scented candle in the bathroom and shower together.
- Tell him five reasons why you love him.
- Turn off the phone, TV, and pager and make him your top priority.
- Unconditionally accept him.
- Scratch your spouse's unreachable itch.
- Compromise cheerfully when necessary.
- View him as God's gift to you.
- Value the things he values.
- Stay open to his feedback and don't become defensive.
- Thank God for your differences—and mean it!

A Chance for Romance

A surprise getaway may add a spark to your fires of romance. You don't have to go far. But you will have to do some advance planning.

Find a spot that you've never stayed in before. Maybe a bed and breakfast inn overlooking a lake or buried deep in the woods. Maybe a motel that boasts in-room fireplaces or whirlpool tubs. Make your reservations early. Ask to see the room you're reserving so that you'll be familiar with its amenities. If possible, pre-pay for one night's lodging so that you will already have the key in your pocket and conveniently avoid the paperwork of check-in when you arrive for your romantic evening.

Enlist the aid of your husband's boss at his office. Ask his boss to give him the day off. Ask a co-worker to cover his meetings or phone calls for him. Throw some toiletry items like toothpaste, aftershave, and shampoo into a small overnight bag. Add your sexiest lingerie and some scented candles. Remember to leave your pager and cell phone at home!

Then, on the day of your getaway, offer to take him to work. Instead of driving to the office, head instead to your romantic getaway spot for that chance for romance.

- Say "no" to your girlfriends' invitation to go shopping, and spend the day with him instead.
- Watch a sunset together.
- Get a new haircut that calls attention to your eyes.
- Smile every time you see him.
- Pray for him.
- If you don't like his faded, ripped flannel shirt, buy him a new one and "distress" it before you give it to him.
- Serenade him with your special song.
- Be impetuous and impractical.
- Wear his favorite perfume.
- Let him take you hunting or fishing, and really try to enjoy it.
- Don't assume that he knows you love him—work to keep love alive!
- Develop a shared interest, activity, or sport.
- Share secrets together.
- Make him your top priority.
- Remember the first time you said, "I love you" to each other.
- Run an errand he hates to do.
- Make him late for breakfast.
- Believe in him.
- Leave love notes in different pockets of his jacket.
- Care about what has happened in his day.
- Convince him to do something silly—just with you.
- Make the coffee the way he likes it.
- Be understanding.
- Laugh at the jokes he tells—even if you've heard them a hundred times.

A Recipe for Love

1 large field
2 people in love
A pinch of brook and some pebbles
A large expanse of deep blue sky
Several kinds of flowers
Warm sunshine
A bathtub of cool water

Mix people well together. Put them in a field, stirring constantly. Pour pebbles into brook, one at a time. Sprinkle flowers over field. Spread blue sky over all. Bake in warm sunshine. When browned and tired, set away in a bathtub of cool water. You will be delighted with the results.

Loving Words

Many waters cannot quench love;
   rivers cannot wash it away.
               SONG OF SONGS 8:7

Jesus said, "Love each other as I have loved you."
               JOHN 15:12

Be devoted to one another in brotherly love.
Honor one another above yourselves.
               ROMANS 12:10

Love covers over all wrongs.
               PROVERBS 10:12

- Learn a new dance step together.
- Place a love note under the windshield wiper of his car.
- Pick up one of his favorite snack foods the next time you're in the grocery store.
- Give him a foot massage.
- Send him flowers.
- Leave him a romantic message on his e-mail.
- Hold his favorite candy bar in your teeth and offer him a bite.
- Send him a note to say thanks for being your friend and soul mate.
- Buy a season ticket to his favorite sport.
- Go to the symphony together.
- Take a cooking class together.
- Learn a hobby that you can do together.
- Do his chores for him without asking or complaining.
- Don't go out of the house with curlers in your hair.
- Throw (or give) away that outfit that he can't stand.
- Plan to grow old together.
- Take turns initiating love-making.
- Go to a new restaurant and experience a new kind of food together.
- Always look your best in public because you are a reflection of his love.
- Spend more time together.
- Give him a hug—just because.
- Buy him a box seat at the ball game.
- Record every check you write in your checkbook.
- Do something unexpected.
- Find ways to be his best friend.

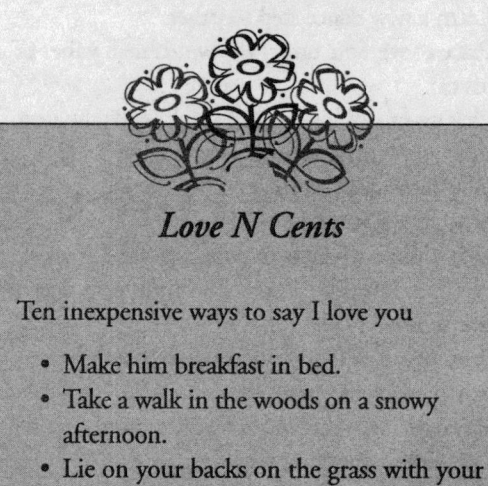

Love N Cents

Ten inexpensive ways to say I love you

- Make him breakfast in bed.
- Take a walk in the woods on a snowy afternoon.
- Lie on your backs on the grass with your heads touching and count the stars.
- Laugh together.
- Rent a video he wants to see and snuggle on the couch.
- Walk his dog.
- Soak in the hot tub together.
- Leave a Hershey's Kiss® on the dashboard of his car (but do this during cool weather or he'll have a chocolate puddle on his dashboard!).
- Catch his eye and give him a sexy wink and a smile.
- Send him a telegram that says, "I love you."

Let Me Count the Ways

Ten reasons why you love him:

- The twinkle in his eye
- The cleft in his chin
- His dimples
- The hair that keeps falling into his eyes
- The arch of his brows
- The curve of his lips
- The wiggle of his nose
- The shape of his ears
- The tilt of his head
- The scratchiness of his beard after a long day

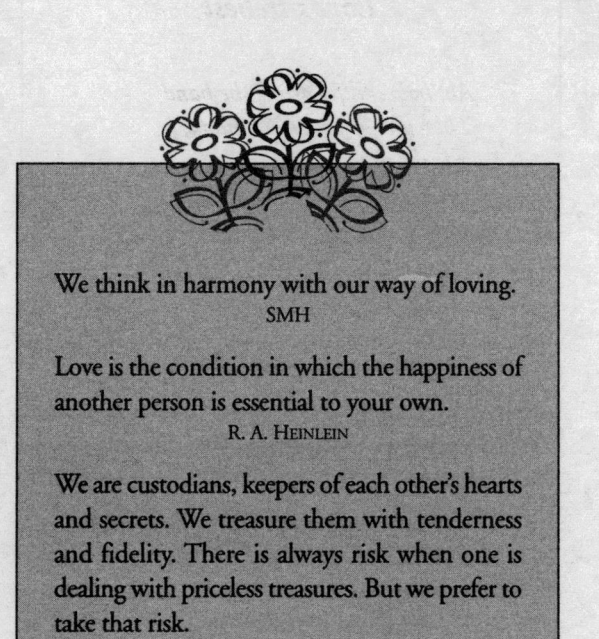

We think in harmony with our way of loving.
SMH

Love is the condition in which the happiness of another person is essential to your own.
R. A. HEINLEIN

We are custodians, keepers of each other's hearts and secrets. We treasure them with tenderness and fidelity. There is always risk when one is dealing with priceless treasures. But we prefer to take that risk.
LIONEL A. WHISTON

Love's Behest

Ah, how skillful grows the hand
That obeyeth love's command,
It is the heart, and not the brain,
That to the highest doth attain,
And he who follows love's behest
Far excelleth all the rest.

AUTHOR UNKNOWN

The Circle

He drew a circle that shut me out,
Heretic, rebel, a thing to flout,
But love and I had a mind to win;
We drew a circle and took him in!

ANONYMOUS

- Never say anything negative about him to anyone else.
- Make up your own nickname for each other.
- Take turns reading aloud together from a favorite book.
- Don't rearrange his toolbox to make it more organized.
- Look for ways to share his load.
- Let him be weak sometimes.
- Cheer him on at bowling league night.
- Learn to ride a horse together.
- Make a crayon portrait of the two of you.
- Whenever he gives you a gift, tell him, "Oh, you shouldn't have!"
- Use every opportunity to applaud him.
- Don't take his favorite car or truck (that he personally waxes twice a week) to the youth group car wash.
- Buy him a gift certificate for a car detailing shop (they'll clean it the way he likes it!).
- Watch him and listen to him to find out what really interests him.
- Keep the cold cream to a minimum when you're together—it could be too frightening for him.
- Don't try to talk seriously about your relationship when the big game is on TV.
- Surprise him with monster truck rally tickets for him and a friend.
- Consider going with him to the monster truck rally.
- Suggest he buy a new cap or T-shirt to commemorate the rally.
- Don't keep a record of how many times you've done the things he wants to do.
- Let him channel surf at least once a day without complaint.
- Remember that a way to a man's heart is through his stomach—feed him well.

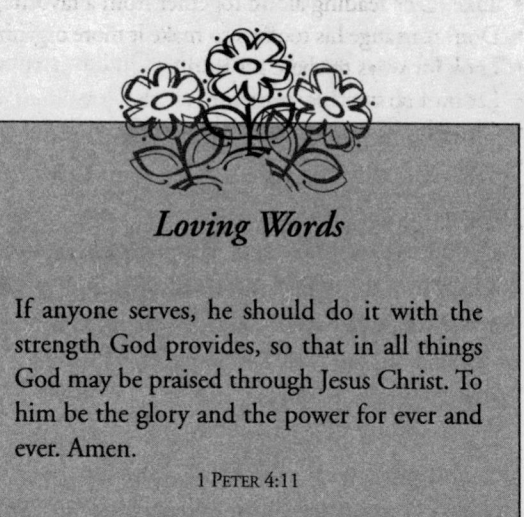

Loving Words

If anyone serves, he should do it with the strength God provides, so that in all things God may be praised through Jesus Christ. To him be the glory and the power for ever and ever. Amen.

1 PETER 4:11

The Lord has told us to love him first and then to love others as much as we love ourselves. That's why true service and surrender go together. Serve by performing the kind of ordinary, menial tasks that meet needs but seldom bring recognition and glory. Any humble chore, when done in Jesus' name, can be a graceful dance of love.

EMILIE BARNES

I Likes It

Several years ago Robertson McQuilkin stepped down from his position as the president of Columbia Bible College and Seminary to care for his wife, Muriel, who suffers from Alzheimer's disease. Dr. McQuilkin writes:

Seventeen summers ago, Muriel and I began our journey into the twilight. It's midnight now, at least for her. Yet, in her silent world, Muriel is so content, so lovable. If Jesus took her home, how I would miss her gentle sweet presence.

Love is said to evaporate if the relationship is not mutual, if it's not physical, if the other person doesn't communicate, or if one party doesn't carry his or her share of the load. When I hear the litany of essentials for a happy marriage, I count off what my beloved can no longer contribute, and I contemplate how truly mysterious love is.

But one night I did reflect. I didn't sleep well and awoke contemplating the puzzle. Muriel was still mobile at that time, so we set out on our morning walk around the block. She wasn't too sure on her feet, so we went slowly and held hands as we always do. This day I heard footsteps behind me and looked back to see the familiar form of a local derelict behind us. He staggered past us, then turned and looked us up and down. "Tha's good." he said. He turned and headed back down the street, mumbling to himself over and over, "Tha's good. I likes it."

When Muriel and I reached our little garden and sat down, his words came back to me. Then the realization hit me; the Lord had spoken through an inebriated old derelict. "It is *you* who are whispering to my spirit, 'I likes it, tha's good.'"

A Time to Remind

Take time to remind him that you love him by looking up the meaning of his name in the back of an unabridged dictionary or in a baby names book. Make a plaque or a poster, monogram a towel or a sweater, etch a stained glass window panel, bake a cake and decorate it with his name and take a photo of it, or in some other way make something permanent that will remind you both of his name and its significance.

Then, whenever you call him by his name, remember the meaning behind that name. Reflect on the qualities hidden in that meaning. Picture him fulfilling the meaning of his name. Be proud of him and call to his attention those times when he lives up to his name and calling.

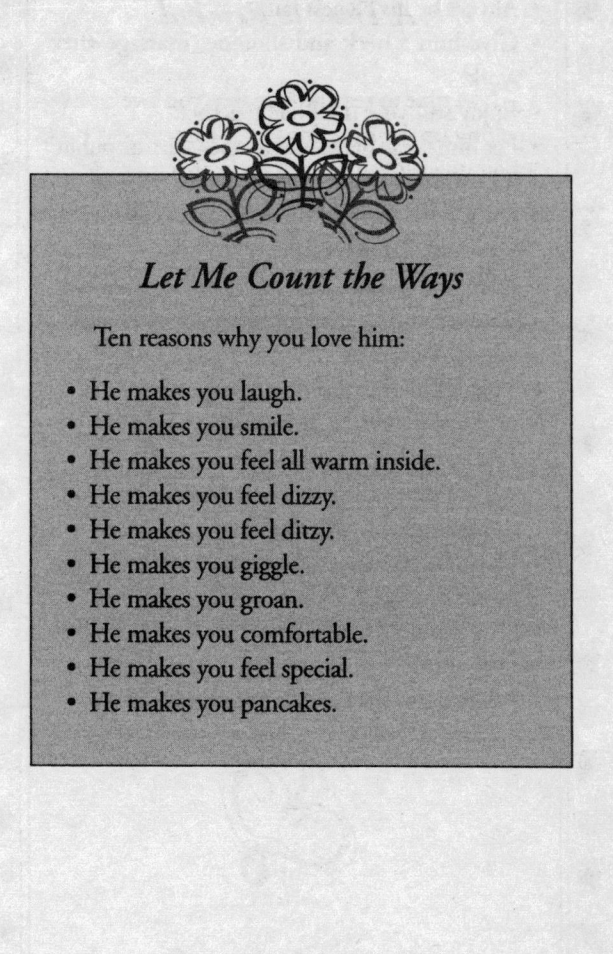

Let Me Count the Ways

Ten reasons why you love him:

- He makes you laugh.
- He makes you smile.
- He makes you feel all warm inside.
- He makes you feel dizzy.
- He makes you feel ditzy.
- He makes you giggle.
- He makes you groan.
- He makes you comfortable.
- He makes you feel special.
- He makes you pancakes.

- Always be his biggest fan.
- Give him a neck and shoulder massage after work.
- Enjoy studying the Bible together.
- Let him wear his stinky flannel shirt in public if he wants to.
- Smell good for him—it may change his mind about the flannel shirt!
- Keep the passion between you so alive that channel surfing is seldom thought of as fulfilling entertainment.
- Thank him for earning a living.
- If he enjoys fishing, learn to gut a fish.
- Encourage him to be a leader.
- Squirrel away some money to surprise him with something he would like.
- Don't laugh when he washes his truck or car motor because it is dusty.
- Serve his needs, because we all want our needs to be met.
- Ask to go to the hardware store with him.

Passionate Pizza

You will need:

1 large prepared pizza crust
1 jar of spaghetti or pizza sauce
1 6-8 oz. package of pepperoni
1 cup diced peppers (red, green, or yellow)
¼ cup diced onion
1 cup shredded mozzarella cheese

Using kitchen scissors, cut the pizza crust into a large heart shape. Spread the sauce onto the heart and layer the prepared ingredients in the order listed, topping the entire pizza with the cheese. Bake in a 375 degree oven for 15-20 minutes until crust is lightly browned and ingredients are warmed. Serve with a smile!

If desired, this pizza can be hand delivered, too. Before assembling your pizza, ask a local pizzeria for an empty pizza box. Then, slip your prepared Passionate Pizza into the box and hand deliver it to your beloved's work place.

A Chance for Romance

To rekindle or keep the fires of romance burning in your relationship, why not recreate your first date or the first time you got together and realized that you liked each other. Set aside some time to go back to the same place and the same spot if possible. If the building, restaurant, or location no longer exists or has changed hands, plan this rendezvous for as nearby as possible or in as similar a setting.

Remember as many things as you can about that date and approximate them again. What did the place look like? What music was playing in the background? What did it smell like? Was it crowded or just the two of you? Was it daytime or nighttime?

What did you have to eat and drink? What did you wear? What did you talk about? How did you get there?

See how many pieces of your first date you can recall and put together. Then, let your sweetie know that you have a wonderful place to go for a date and surprise him with this memory and chance for romance.

Don't bypass the potential for meaningful relationships just because of differences. Explore them. Embrace them. Love them.

LUCI SWINDOLL

Love neither set the planets on their course nor hung the moon in the sky, yet it seems to make the world go 'round.
Though weary, love is not tired;
Though pressed, it is not straightened;
Though alarmed, it is not confounded.
Love securely passes through all.

THOMAS À KEMPIS

Love is like a tranquil breeze that sweeps over my soul making me whole.

AUTHOR UNKNOWN

Love is the emblem of eternity; it confounds all notion of time; effaces all memory of beginning, all fear of an end.

MADAME DE STAEL

- Attend church together.
- Take a walk together and don't talk—just hold hands and enjoy each other's company.
- Let him sit in your favorite chair for a change.
- Get him a new kitchen gadget he can use when you're not around to help fix supper.
- Share an umbrella on a rainy day.
- Let him name one of the pets with a serious name like "Killer" or "Kid Vicious."
- Bring home flowers for him unexpectedly—guys like to receive flowers, too.
- Let him win a snowball fight.
- Let him teach you to play paint ball for the fun of it.
- Go to an ice hockey game instead of "Stars on Ice."
- Get up with the kids or pets and let him sleep in.
- Let him drive your car.
- Sweep out the garage.
- Sit and watch bass fishing or golf programs with him.
- If you don't like the outfit he's wearing, buy him another one.
- Use openly the first handmade anything he makes for you—whether it's a clunky jewelry box of Popsicle sticks or a hand-carved replica of the Jolly Green Giant to hold your rings while washing the dishes.
- Remove your nylons and fine washables from the bathroom before he goes in to use it.

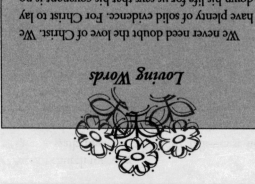

Loving Words

We never need doubt the love of Christ. We have plenty of solid evidence. For Christ to lay down his life for us says that his covenant is no schoolboy pledge or head-of-state agreement or legal contract. Christ's love emanates powerful emotion. For him to die for you is for him to be delighted in you.

I can't keep such good news to myself. When you're in love, one thing's for certain: you tell others about it. We are happier and more complete when we express our love for God to others.

So take time to enjoy the Lover of your soul. Feel the overflow of his love for you. Let Christ's passion for you stir the depths of your yearnings for him. Let yourself be drawn to him today, not only because of his sacrifice for your sin, but because of his desire for your soul. After all, as it says in 1 John 4:19: "We love because he first loved us."

JONI EARECKSON TADA

You

When I deserve your love the least, that's when you give
    it the most.
When I'm irritable, exhausted, discouraged, or distant,
    you understand.
You make me want to do nice things for everybody in my
    path.
And then I like myself better for that.
    I guess you could say
    your love multiplies me.
Variety is nice—in games, in music, in tasks.
But you provide all the "spice" I need in life.
You have all the ingredients
    for my favorite recipe of love.

DIANNA BOOHER

A Time to Remind

Take a moment to remind him of the reasons you fell in love with him:

- The way he reached for your hand
- The way he said "Good night"
- His concern for your pets
- His understanding heart
- His giving nature
- His ability to see the good things in you
- His trust in you
- His uncompromising honesty
- His love for others
- His love for God

Loving Him

Use this page to record your feelings about your love for him:

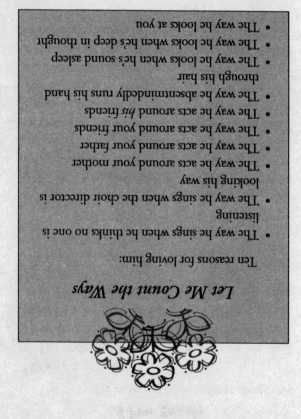

Let Me Count the Ways

Ten reasons for loving him:

- The way he sings when he thinks no one is listening
- The way he sings when the choir director is looking his way
- The way he acts around your mother
- The way he acts around your father
- The way he acts around your friends
- The way he acts around *his* friends
- The way he absentmindedly runs his hand through his hair
- The way he looks when he's sound asleep
- The way he looks when he's deep in thought
- The way he looks at you

A Pen Speaks

My very dear Sarah,

The indications are very strong that we shall move in a few days—perhaps tomorrow. Lest I should not be able to write again, I feel impelled to write a few lines that may fall under your eye when I shall be no more.

I have, I know, but few and small claims upon Divine Providence, but something whispers to me … that I shall return to my loved ones unharmed. If I do not, my dear Sarah, never forget how much I love you, and when my last breath escapes me on the battlefield, it will whisper your name.

But, O Sarah! if the dead can come back to this earth and flit unseen around those they loved, I shall always be near you; in the gladdest days and in the darkest nights … *always, always*, and if there be a soft breeze upon your cheek, it shall be my breath; as the cool air fans your throbbing temple, it shall be my spirit passing by.

Confederate soldier Major Sullivan Ballou wrote this letter to his beloved wife on July 14, 1861. Seven days later, he was killed in battle.

Are there words of love you could say to your sweetheart that should not be left unsaid? You could make a telephone call to him and tell him how much you love him. While a telephone call is wonderful, it doesn't have the lasting impact of a letter written from the heart. The warm feeling and lovely memory of the call can swiftly fade. A letter, on the other hand, is a more permanent record of your feelings. It can be read again and again, warming the heart each time.

Love letters give us the opportunity to relive the joys of love and romance. As Richard Exley has said, love letters "remain, as always, love's most enduring expression."

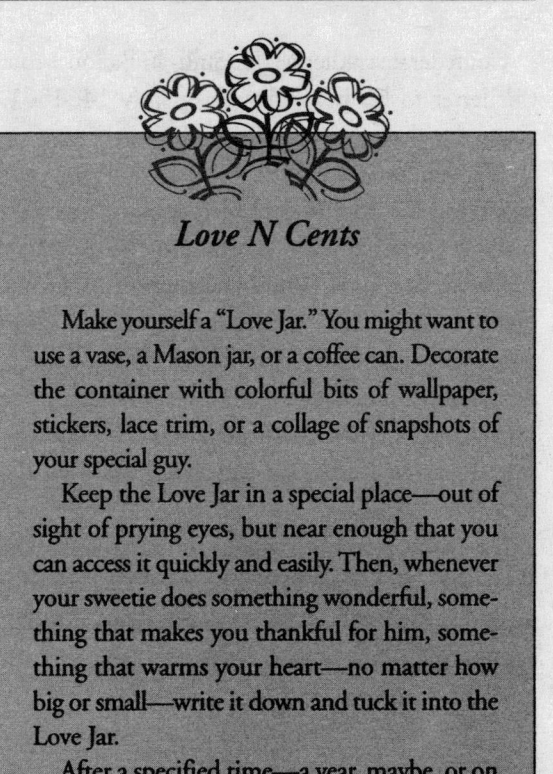

Love N Cents

Make yourself a "Love Jar." You might want to use a vase, a Mason jar, or a coffee can. Decorate the container with colorful bits of wallpaper, stickers, lace trim, or a collage of snapshots of your special guy.

Keep the Love Jar in a special place—out of sight of prying eyes, but near enough that you can access it quickly and easily. Then, whenever your sweetie does something wonderful, something that makes you thankful for him, something that warms your heart—no matter how big or small—write it down and tuck it into the Love Jar.

After a specified time—a year, maybe, or on your anniversary or when he needs a real pick-me-up—pull out the Love Jar and read the things you've written down together. He'll be able to see himself through your eyes as you remember lots of reasons why you love him.

The Fruit of the Spirit

Galatians 5:22–23 says: "The fruit of the Spirit is love, joy, peace, patience, kindness, goodness, faithfulness, gentleness and self-control." Notice that love is the first fruit mentioned. That's because love is the key to all of the other fruits of the Spirit.

About these verses, Donald Grey Barnhouse observed, "Love is the key. Joy is love singing. Peace is love resting. Long-suffering (patience) is love enduring. Kindness is love's touch. Goodness is love's character. Faithfulness is love's habit. Gentleness is love's self-forgetfulness. Self-control is love holding the reins."

May your love exhibit all the fruit of the Spirit in all its facets!

- Remember that in tough times he may just want the comfort of your hug.
- Remember the promises you've made to him—whether marriage vows or otherwise—and keep them.
- Plan time to give to the community together—at a homeless shelter, serving food in a mission kitchen, or helping in a food distribution program.
- Like the outfit he bought you.
- Take out the trash even though it's his chore.
- Listen to him when he offers helpful criticisms.
- Don't gripe whenever his friends come over and invade the house.
- Clean out your closet before you clean out the kitchen cupboards.
- Find an unexplored path and explore it together.
- Ask him what he would like to do for your next vacation—and cheerfully do it.
- Hug more than you talk.
- Buy his "toys" before you buy yours.
- Never, never, never give a job jar as a Valentine's Day gift.
- Don't get upset when he doesn't understand why you're crying about a McDonald's commercial—ask for a hug instead.
- Let him win the "tickle" war.
- Compliment his father.
- Don't keep changing and changing your outfits while he's been waiting for you to go out. Pick one, and stick with it.
- Pick it up (whatever it is) and put it in the hamper.
- Follow his suggestions when you are sick.

An Old-Fashioned Love Song

Wander the web, haunt a library, browse in a music store, paw through a box of old LPs, and see if you can locate the words and music to one of these old-fashioned love songs. Listen to it, learn it, and sing it to your beloved. Your voice may not be ready for the Met, but your voice is the one your beloved wants to hear singing a heartfelt song of love. Here are some titles to find:

"They Can't Take That Away From Me,"
   George Gershwin
"As Time Goes By," from the movie *Casablanca*
"Smoke Gets in Your Eyes," The Platters
"Unforgettable," Nat King Cole
"Chances Are," Johnny Mathis
"Our Love is Here to Stay," George Gershwin

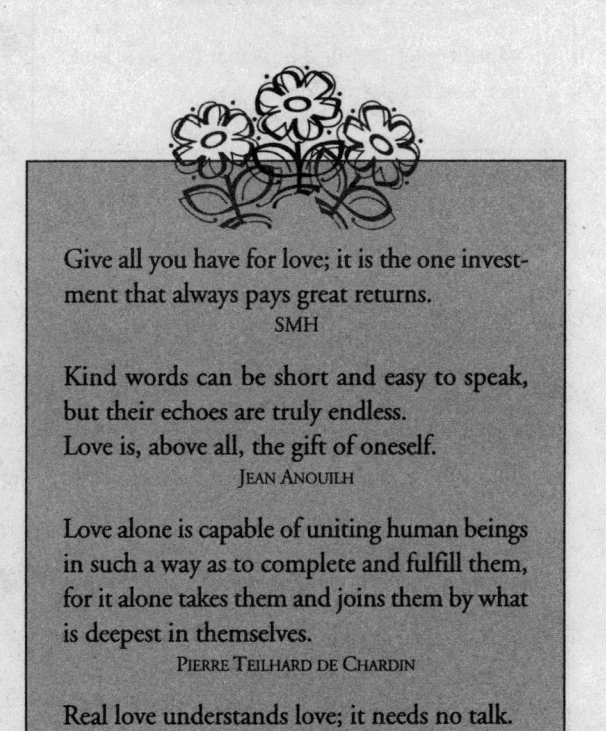

Give all you have for love; it is the one invest-
ment that always pays great returns.
SMH

Kind words can be short and easy to speak,
but their echoes are truly endless.
Love is, above all, the gift of oneself.
JEAN ANOUILH

Love alone is capable of uniting human beings
in such a way as to complete and fulfill them,
for it alone takes them and joins them by what
is deepest in themselves.
PIERRE TEILHARD DE CHARDIN

Real love understands love; it needs no talk.
F. R. HAVERGAL

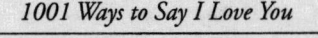
A Time to Remind

Take time to remind him that you love him when you thank him for:

- falling in love with you
- believing in you
- his gentle touch
- being the best hugger in the world
- the way he holds you tight
- his emotional support
- being there through the good times and the bad
- teaching you what love is really all about
- being an awesome friend
- putting up with you

- Hold hands when standing in line.
- Slip a love note into the pocket of his jeans where he keeps his wallet.
- Pray for him every day.
- Have your picture taken professionally and put the photo in a unique frame just for him.
- Keep a scrapbook of just you two and the things you do together.
- Write a letter to his mother and thank her for raising such a wonderful son.
- Send an "unbirthday" card.
- Give him a kind word or compliment.
- Give him a peck on the cheek in a crowded elevator and tell him you love him.
- Rent a stretch limo for a few hours on his birthday and drive past his friends' homes.
- Be the first to say "I'm sorry."
- Love him so much that romance novels could be written about you.
- Give him a monogrammed blanket that you can use to snuggle in.
- Kiss every time you cross a state line.
- Believe him when he says, "I wouldn't wear that outfit if I were you."
- Know that when your mall search for the perfect outfit has taken four hours, it's time to call it quits.
- When tax time comes, don't assume that either one of you knows what you're doing.
- Remember the date of the first time you said, "I love you," and let that warmth fill your heart again.

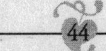

Let Me Count the Ways

Ten reasons why you love him:

- He's loving
- He's attentive
- He's romantic
- He's handsome
- He's intelligent
- He's sexy
- He's confident
- He's independent
- He's caring
- He has a wonderful sense of humor

Just Wanted You to Know

The story is told of a salesman who called his wife from a coin-operated telephone in a distant city. He finished the conversation, told his wife how much he missed her, and said good-bye. He replaced the receiver and turned to go, but as he was walking away the telephone began to ring.

The salesman went back and answered the telephone, expecting to be informed of some extra charges. Instead the operator said, "I thought you'd like to know. Just after you hung up, your wife said, 'I love you.'"

ADAPTED FROM JAMES HEWETT

- Make sure you know how he pays the bills so you don't have to worry about the future.
- Smile when the one you love enters the room.
- Call or page him unexpectedly just to tell him you love him.
- Change something in your decorating scheme to show him you care—move his picture by your chair, etc.
- Call a local radio station and dedicate a song to him.
- Decorate the house with balloons—one for every month you've known him.
- Turn to him in public and whisper, "On a scale of 1 to 10, you're a 12!"
- Kiss the palm of his hand, close his fingers into a fist, and say, "Save this!"
- Make fun a part of your life.
- Buy him a new pair of gym socks.
- Give him a shopping spree—just for the fun of it.
- Don't expect anything back when you fix him a nice dinner.
- Live happily ever after.
- Take time together to listen to church bells or carillons as they ring out songs of praise to God.
- Believe in each other.
- Use one of his pet names as your ATM password.
- Remember that appearances can deceive: don't just love his looks.
- Ask him how you could help him with a project.
- Always be kind.
- Consider that seven dogs may be going a bit overboard for companionship.
- Love God first—then loving him will come naturally

A Chance for Romance

Childhood field trips to the zoo, museum, or aquarium were always an enjoyable break from routine. But why should kids have all the fun? A day or a weekend trip to a local museum, aquarium, or zoo can be a chance for romance, too. Check out travel and tour books or ask your local library to find some of the best sites in your area.

Pack a picnic lunch to enjoy, and be a little silly as you wander through the exhibits—laughter will lighten your heart and get you in a loving mood. Mimic the animals in the zoo. Flap and wiggle like the penguins at the aquarium. Play with the hands-on exhibits in the museum.

To alert your sweetheart to the trip, place a little plastic animal, fish, or dime store gem in a small gift box. Add a note that says: "You're such a great catch (or "find"). How about a trip to the aquarium (or zoo or museum) this weekend?

Love is the strange bewilderment which overtakes one person on account of another person.
AUTHOR UNKNOWN

Love doesn't sit back and snooze. It is not apathetic. It is ready and willing. It is neither passive nor indifferent. It refuses to yawn its way through life. Authentic love is demonstrative, not sterile and dull.
CHARLES SWINDOLL

There are some people with such a lofty conception of love that they never succeed in expressing it in the simple kindnesses of ordinary life.
PAUL TOURNIER

You can give without loving, but you cannot love without giving.
AMY CARMICHAEL

Only true love gives more than it ever expects to receive.
SMH

- Remember courtesy is *not* dead. Say please and thank you; carry yourself with grace and beauty; be a lady.
- Go a complete day without getting angry.
- Learn the art of giving a massage.
- Sing your special song to each other.
- Talk about the songs that have meant a lot to you over the years.
- Share prayer needs with each other.
- Talk about the differences and similarities in your faith and worship styles.
- Go to Sunday school together.
- Tell him about a dream or goal you would like to one day achieve.
- Ask him what his favorite color is.
- Ask him what he most likes to eat.
- Ask him where he would most like to live.
- Ask him what he would most like to do if money were no object.
- Surprise him with spontaneous gifts like candy, a new key chain, or a grocery store bouquet.
- Learn a few magic or card tricks to share with him.
- Take him with you to go back and visit your birthplace.
- Buy his favorite flavor of seedless jam.
- Run a cross-country race together.
- Spend an afternoon in a used book store and look for a book you can read aloud to each other.
- Concentrate on communicating openly with him 50 percent better than you did last week.
- Order a bouquet of balloons to be delivered to his work place.

Loving Words

Two are better than one, because they have a
good return for their work:
If one falls down, his friend can help him up.
ECCLESIASTES 4:9–10

I belong to my lover,
and his desire is for me.
SONG OF SONGS 7:10

Place me like a seal over your heart,
like a seal on your arm;
for love is as strong as death.
SONG OF SONGS 8:6

May God give you the desire of your heart
and make all your plans succeed.
PSALM 20:4

- Plan a dream vacation.
- Always have one set of tickets to an upcoming event tacked to your bulletin board.
- Make flags from toothpicks and tiny squares of paper with tiny love notes written on them; stick them where he will see them—in his food, on his dash, on his desk or dresser.
- Schedule a lunch meeting once a month for the two of you.
- At Christmas time, tie yourself up in a big, red bow and wait for him under the Christmas tree.
- Order pizza for him and have it delivered to his office when he has to work late.
- Help him conquer one of his fears.
- Send a thank you card to him every day for an entire week; be specific in your gratitude.
- Help him break one bad habit this year.
- Give him one sincere compliment every day for a week.
- Be forgiving.
- Spend more time with him than surfing on the web.
- Make a greeting card as tall as the room that says "I love you."
- Visit a national park together and learn about its significance.
- Memorize each other's favorite passage of Scripture.

A Time to Remind

Why not work in the garden together and raise flowers or vegetables to share with others. You can make your gardening time a togetherness time. The time spent preparing the soil can be a time of sharing and talking together about your cares and concerns.

As you plant the seeds, you can pray together that God will bless your garden with a good harvest and your relationship with a renewed sense of growth. As you water the garden and soak the roots of the seedlings, you can have a water fight and soak each other with laughter and silliness.

As you pull the weeds and mulch around the plants, you can confess the hurts and problems that have sprung up like weeds in your relationship. And when the harvest is ready, you can reap the benefits of your labor, both from the garden and from your renewed relationship.

Cookie Monster

You will need:

1 cup chocolate chips
½ cup brown sugar
¾ cup granulated sugar
1 ¼ cup quick cooking oatmeal
1 cup flour
½ teaspoon baking powder
½ teaspoon baking soda
¼ teaspoon salt

Assemble these ingredients in the order listed from top to bottom in a quart jar. Top with a decorative piece of fabric or a colorful sticker. Write the following recipe on a label and affix it to the front of the jar:

"For my cookie monster, here's a quick way to bake some cookies. You will need to melt one stick of butter and blend it with 1¼ teaspoons of vanilla extract. Then stir in the contents of this jar. Spoon out golf ball sized lumps of dough and bake them on a cookie sheet in a 375 degree oven for 12 to 15 minutes. If you'll let me know when the cookies are done, I'll come help you eat them, too."

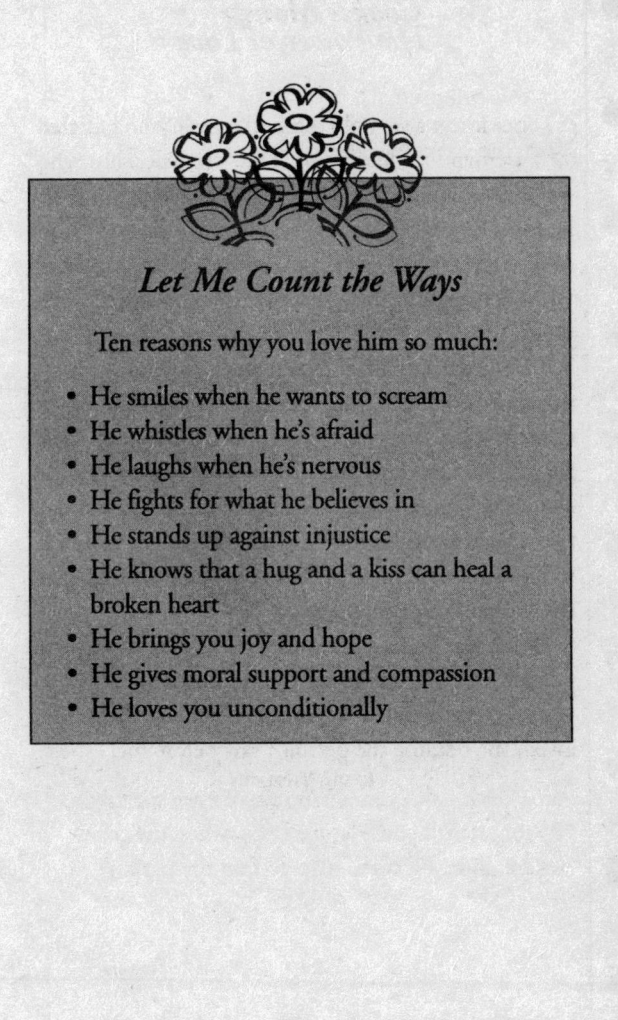

Let Me Count the Ways

Ten reasons why you love him so much:

- He smiles when he wants to scream
- He whistles when he's afraid
- He laughs when he's nervous
- He fights for what he believes in
- He stands up against injustice
- He knows that a hug and a kiss can heal a broken heart
- He brings you joy and hope
- He gives moral support and compassion
- He loves you unconditionally

The Power of Love

I once knew a very old married couple who radiated a tremendous happiness. The wife especially, who was almost unable to move because of old age and illness and in whose kind old face the joys and sufferings of many years had etched a hundred lines, was filled with such a gratitude for life that I was touched to the quick.

Involuntarily, I asked myself what could possibly be the source of this kindly person's radiance. In every other respect they were common people, and their room indicated only the most modest comfort. But suddenly I knew where it all came from. I saw those two speaking to each other, and their eyes hanging upon each other. All at once it became clear to me that this woman was dearly loved.

It was not because she was a cheerful and pleasant person that she was loved by her husband all those years. It was the other way around. Because she was so loved, she became the person I saw before me.

HELMUT THIELICKE

Love Notes

My greatest good fortune in a life of brilliant experience has been to find you, and to lead my life with you. I don't feel far away from you out here at all. I feel very near in my heart: and also I feel that the nearer I get to honour, the nearer I am to you.

WINSTON CHURCHILL TO HIS WIFE, CLEMENTINE

Already the second day since our marriage, his love and gentleness is beyond everything, and to kiss that dear soft cheek, to press my lips to his, is heavenly bliss. I feel a purer more unearthly feeling than I ever did. Oh! Was ever a woman so blessed as I am.

QUEEN VICTORIA, FEBRUARY 12, 1840, JOURNAL ENTRY

The way you let your hand rest in mine, my bewitching Sweetheart, fills me with happiness. It is the perfection of confiding love. Everything you do, the little unconscious things in particular, charms me and increases my sense of nearness to you, identification with you, till my heart is full to overflowing.

WOODROW WILSON, TO HIS WIFE

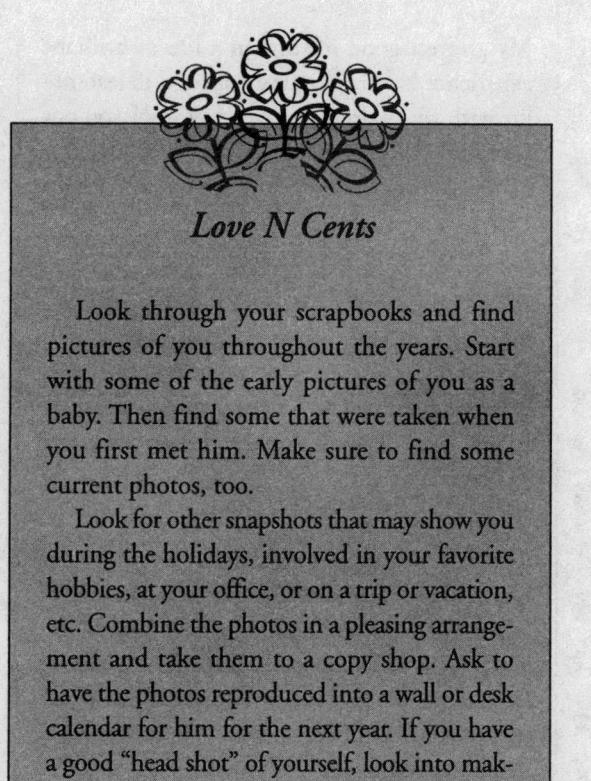

Love N Cents

Look through your scrapbooks and find pictures of you throughout the years. Start with some of the early pictures of you as a baby. Then find some that were taken when you first met him. Make sure to find some current photos, too.

Look for other snapshots that may show you during the holidays, involved in your favorite hobbies, at your office, or on a trip or vacation, etc. Combine the photos in a pleasing arrangement and take them to a copy shop. Ask to have the photos reproduced into a wall or desk calendar for him for the next year. If you have a good "head shot" of yourself, look into making that into a mouse pad for his office or home computer station.

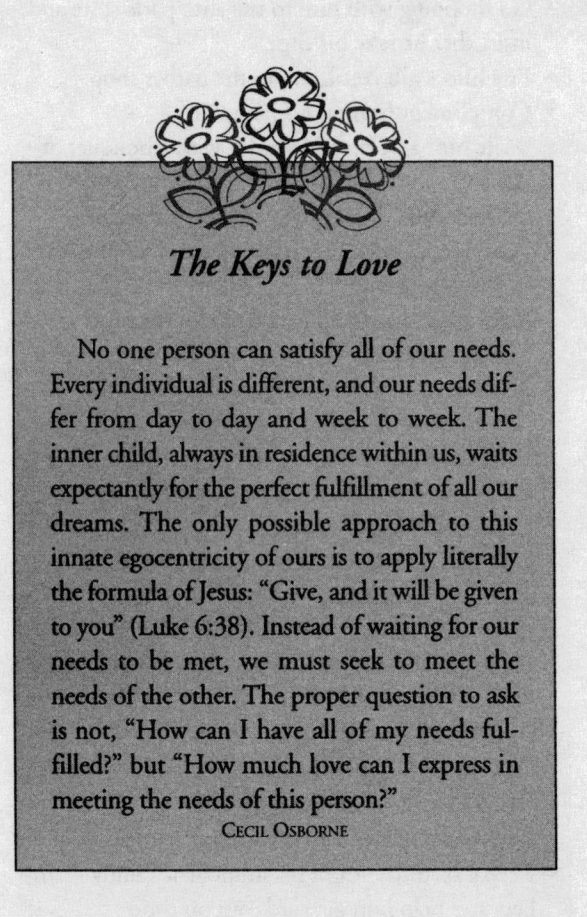

The Keys to Love

No one person can satisfy all of our needs. Every individual is different, and our needs differ from day to day and week to week. The inner child, always in residence within us, waits expectantly for the perfect fulfillment of all our dreams. The only possible approach to this innate egocentricity of ours is to apply literally the formula of Jesus: "Give, and it will be given to you" (Luke 6:38). Instead of waiting for our needs to be met, we must seek to meet the needs of the other. The proper question to ask is not, "How can I have all of my needs fulfilled?" but "How much love can I express in meeting the needs of this person?"

CECIL OSBORNE

- Go shopping with him to the auto parts store and insist that he take his time.
- Buy him a gift certificate to the barber shop.
- Compliment him on his new shirt.
- Write him a poem and send it with a bouquet of flowers.
- Let him show you how to cook a new recipe.
- Rent a canoe on a moonlit night and sail the seas of love together.
- Remember that romance isn't just a weekend sport.
- Kiss in at least five different states in the next year.
- Be 30 percent more loving for the next 30 days.
- Remember that staying in love requires consistent action and a conscious decision.
- Go to an adult education class together.
- Create a "romance" category in your budget.
- Give him a $100 gift certificate to his favorite sporting goods store.
- Show you care with a tender kiss.
- Write notes to his parents to tell them what you've been doing together.
- Visit his relatives with him.
- On Mother's Day or Father's Day send his folks a card, thanking them for their son.
- Call his mother just to say hello.
- Keep a birthday list of his immediate family members and help him get cards out on time.
- Ask his mother for the recipe to his favorite dessert.
- Ask God to give you a spirit of love and thankfulness for his family.

I Love You

I love you
For the part of me
That you bring out;
I love you
For putting your hand
Into my heaped-up heart
And passing over
All the foolish, weak things
That you can't help
Dimly seeing there,
And for drawing out
Into the light
All the beautiful belongings
That no one else had looked
Quite far enough to find.

I love you because you
Are helping me to make
Of the lumber of my life
Not a tavern
But a temple;
Out of the works
Of my every day
Not a reproach
But a song ...

AUTHOR UNKNOWN

- Compliment him in public in front of his friends or peers.
- Hire a barbershop quartet to sing "Happy Birthday" to him.
- Flash a love message on a hotel or ballpark's signboard.
- If you fight about the same thing over and over again, get to the root of the problem once and for all.
- Go to a drive-in movie together.
- After you've talked on the phone, call him back in a few minutes to tell him how much you miss him.
- On his birthday, make a special display of his baby pictures with the phrase "You must have been a beautiful baby, 'cause baby look at you now!"
- Purposely hold hands when his family is watching.
- Purposely give him a lingering glance in public.
- Sometimes wait for him to arrive by sitting on the front steps; smile as he comes up the walk.
- Back him in his decisions.
- Be honest in your communication.
- Just once ask, "What can I do to make you happier?"
- Praise his accomplishments to others who come to visit.
- Appreciate him.
- Be willing to do whatever he asks without grumbling.
- Brag enthusiastically about him.
- Never betray his confidences—keep his secrets.
- Never speak to him with a bitter tone.
- Remember that griping and complaining only leads to resentment—do all things without murmuring or complaining.
- Never apologize for him in public.
- Nurture him in as many ways as possible.

Something Happened to My Heart

Something happened to my heart
The day when I met you,
Something strange and wonderful.
Skies above were blue.

Steeple bells began to chime,
Birds began to sing,
Flowers popped up everywhere;
Suddenly, glad spring!

Something happened to my heart!
Now I know you're mine;
Our love shall be endless, dear,
The perfect valentine!

GEORGIA B. ADAMS

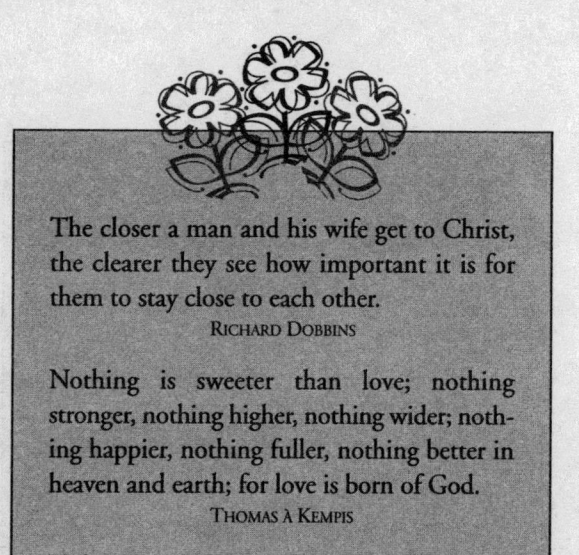

The closer a man and his wife get to Christ, the clearer they see how important it is for them to stay close to each other.
RICHARD DOBBINS

Nothing is sweeter than love; nothing stronger, nothing higher, nothing wider; nothing happier, nothing fuller, nothing better in heaven and earth; for love is born of God.
THOMAS À KEMPIS

To love is to believe, to hope, to know;
'tis an essay, a taste of heaven below.
EDMUND WALLER

Love is rewarded with deepening affection and countless shy glances.
SMH

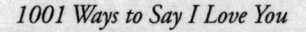

Let Me Count the Ways

I love him even when:

- He endlessly channel surfs
- He forgets to take the trash out
- He talks endlessly about his car
- He forgets to let the dog out
- He buys more tools
- He still wears the same old shirt
- He wants to go camping, again
- He forgets to hug and only talks
- He is without a doubt himself!

Married Life

Natural reason looks at married life, turns up her nose and says: "Why must I rock the baby, wash its diapers, change its bed, smell its odor, heal its rash, take care of this and take care of that, do this and do that? It is better to remain single and live a quiet and carefree life."

But what does the Christian faith say? The father opens his eyes, looks at these lowly, distasteful, and despised things and knows that they are adorned with divine approval as with the most precious gold and silver. God, with his angels and creatures, will smile—not because diapers are washed, but because it is done in faith.

MARTIN LUTHER

- Take the day off and become his "servant for the day" doing whatever he wants.
- Send him a giant chocolate chip cookie made in the shape of a heart.
- Have a 5-course meal sent to him at work for lunch.
- Have a photo calendar made with all of his favorite photos.
- Send him a different CD of love songs each day for a week.
- Make silly pictures at a "4-for-a-dollar" photo machine and have them framed.
- Send him a reminder card that expresses your undying love and affection.
- Take a hayride on an autumn afternoon.
- Go Christmas shopping together in the middle of July.
- Play hide and seek in the dark.
- Keep his favorite flavor of ice cream in the freezer at all times.
- Remember that chocolate is always the right choice when saying I love you.
- Try expressing your love through the delivery of a single rose in a crystal bud vase.
- Tell him you love him, without saying a word.
- Love him by letting him sit in your arms without saying much of anything.
- Sit quietly by the fire and tell him all the things you adore about him.
- Take him to the edge of town late at night to look for shooting stars together.
- Send him a heart cut out of construction paper with your names written on it in crayon.
- Reach over and take his hand during church.
- Buy a Valentine card in February and send it to him in October.

- Have his favorite magazine waiting for him in his chair.
- Suggest he invite his parents over for supper.
- Hide little gifts around the house for him in places only he will look and find.
- Learn as much as you can about his work.
- Wake him gently with a kiss.
- Be cheerful even when you don't feel that way.
- Give him some private time for hobbies, friends, and time alone.
- Build a snowman together.
- Wash the car together.
- Agree on a place you would like to go together. Put a piggy bank in an accessible place to begin saving for the trip.
- Use the word "ours" instead of "mine" whenever you can.
- Never ask him to do something you can do for yourself.
- Never compare him with old boyfriends, not even in good ways.
- Make the date of the month that you met a special day every month thereafter.
- Remind him that he belongs to God.
- Exchange back scratches.
- If he brings work home from the office, ask if you can help.
- Put his phone number in the #1 speed dial position on your work phone.
- Keep a joint journal in which you both can write.
- Be proud of him and show it at family reunions.
- Shop with him for a new golf club.
- Bring home his favorite kind of bagel.

Loving Him

Use this page to record your feelings about your love for him:

_____

_____

_____

_____

_____

_____

_____

_____

_____

_____

_____

_____

_____

_____

_____

_____

_____

_____

_____

_____

_____

Loving Words

Love always protects, always trusts, always hopes, always perseveres.

1 CORINTHIANS 13:7

We know and rely on the love God has for us. God is love.

1 JOHN 4:16

May the Lord direct your hearts into God's love and Christ's perseverance.

2 THESSALONIANS 3:5

Surely goodness and love will follow me all the days of my life, and I will dwell in the house of the LORD forever.

PSALM 23:6

Card Tricks

Make him a personalized greeting card every day this week. Leave it in a different place each time. Here are some quotes you might want to use for the inside greeting, or make up some of your own:

I would love to spend all my time writing to you; I'd love to share with you all that goes through my mind, all that weighs on my heart, all that gives air to my soul.

LUIGI PIRANDELLO

Love can never grow old.
Locks may lose their brown and gold.
Cheeks may fade and hollow grow.
But the hearts that love, will know
never winter's frost and chill;
summer's warmth is in them still.

LEO BUSCAGLIA

Somewhere there's a someone who dreams of your
   smile,
And finds in your presence that life is worthwhile.
So when you are lonely, remember this is true:
Somebody, somewhere is thinking of you.

AUTHOR UNKNOWN

A Time to Remind

Remind him you love him when you ask about his family heritage and try to learn all you can about his roots. Every nationality is rich in customs, folklore, and family traditions.

Ask him about his ancestors. Find out about the family customs and traditions that accompany the holidays. Incorporate as many of his family traditions, customs, foods, and folklore that you can into your relationship. Visit a museum or heritage exhibit to learn more about his background.

All of these pieces of his past have helped make him into the person he is today. Appreciate him for his diversity, for his heritage, for all that he is.

Faith goes up the stairs that love has made and looks out of the windows which hope has opened.

CHARLES SPURGEON

The law of love can never be a cherishing of self at the expense of the loved one, but must always be the cherishing of the loved one at the expense of self.

HANNAH WHITALL SMITH

Love strives toward more than it attains.

THOMAS À KEMPIS

Two cannot go in opposite directions if they are in love—love shares a direction of vision.

SMH

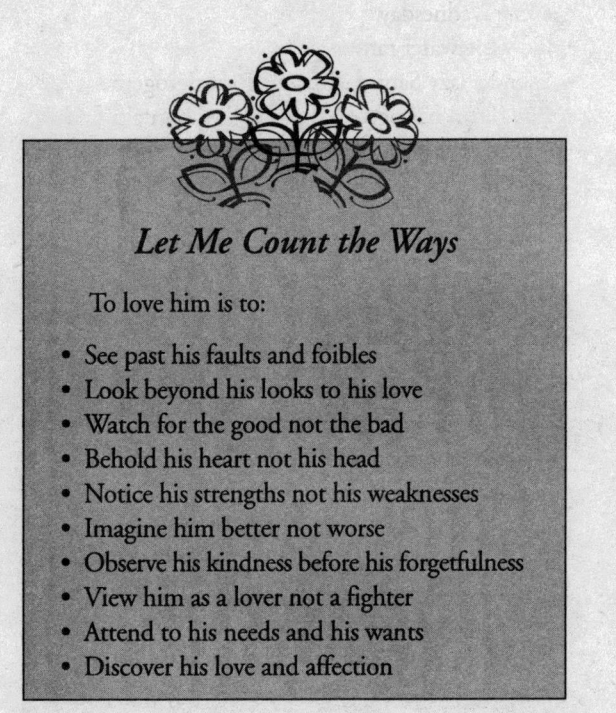

Let Me Count the Ways

To love him is to:

- See past his faults and foibles
- Look beyond his looks to his love
- Watch for the good not the bad
- Behold his heart not his head
- Notice his strengths not his weaknesses
- Imagine him better not worse
- Observe his kindness before his forgetfulness
- View him as a lover not a fighter
- Attend to his needs and his wants
- Discover his love and affection

- Make your own rituals like giving him a little gift every Wednesday.
- Go whitewater rafting.
- Spend a lazy Saturday in a hammock together.
- Buy him a bar of soap that smells mountain fresh.
- Offer to take care of the kids (yours or the ones he's responsible for—nieces, nephews, neighbors, etc.) so that he can have some time alone.
- Send him a FedEx letter that says "I love you."
- Kiss on a chairlift.
- Never watch TV during dinner.
- Help take the cars to the repair shop.
- Always maintain eye contact when complimenting him.
- Avoid discussions of work, finances, parents, children, or church problems during romantic times.
- Go to the mall and don't charge anything.
- Frame several of the greeting cards he has sent you into a collage of love.
- Kiss his hands while he is reading.
- Buy him black silk boxer shorts.
- Leave a note asking, "Can we get away this weekend—just you and me?"
- Make a tape-recorded love letter for him.
- Don't neglect your relationship because the girls want to go out.
- Leave a love letter in an unexpected place—pinned to the inside of his shirt, tucked into his lunch bag, crushed into the toe of a shoe, etc.
- Massage his temples when he has a headache.

In the arithmetic of love, one plus one equals
everything, and two minus one equals nothing.
MIGNON MCLAUGHLIN

Love takes two.
UNKNOWN

To love anyone is nothing else than to wish
that person good.
ST. THOMAS AQUINAS

Make this the chief desire of your love: to link
yourself week by week by bonds which shall
ever become more intimate.

Love is hundreds of tiny threads which sew
people together through the years.
SIMONE SIGNORET

Love N Cents

See how many ways in one day you can find to surprise him by doing something for him that he always does. Here are some ideas to get your started. Add more ideas of your own and make your own love list.

Make Saturday morning breakfast

Water the lawn

Check the oil in the car

Fill the gas tank with gasoline

Shovel the snow from the walk

Unload the dishwasher

Run the errands to the bank and post office

Set up a babysitter for your next date

- Learn how to say "I love you" in a foreign language and leave it on his voice mail.
- Treat him to a triple scoop cone of his favorite ice cream.
- Budget money regularly for fun.
- Balance the checkbook as soon as the statement arrives.
- Flirt with him at a party.
- Carry a lock of his hair in your wallet.
- Offer to drive for a bit on a long distance trip.
- Screen his phone calls for him when he is tired; tell folks he'll call them back.
- Make a crazy little gift for him for no reason—a painted rock for a paperweight, etc.
- Serve breakfast to him and his friends before they go off for a day of fishing.
- Thank him for all the good times.
- Spell out his name in Christmas tree lights.
- Don't put your relationship on hold because there's a sale at Nordstrom's.
- Thank him for persevering through the bad times with you.
- Send a bouquet made of little love notes fashioned into flowers.
- Create a fill-in-the-blanks love letter for him.
- Write "I love you" on a cake with icing.
- Chalk a cryptic love message on the driveway.
- Tape a love note to the inside of his closet door.
- During a winter walk, surprise him with a thermos of hot cocoa.
- Make him a custom gingerbread man for Christmas.

The Bell

A story is told in England that at the time of Oliver Cromwell a young soldier was tried in military court and sentenced to death. He was to be shot at the "ringing of the curfew bell."

His fiancé climbed up into the bell tower several hours before curfew time and tied herself to the bell's huge clapper. At curfew time, when only muted sounds came out of the bell tower, Cromwell demanded to know why the bell was not ringing. His soldiers went to investigate and found the young woman cut and bleeding from being knocked back and forth against the great bell.

They brought her down, and the story goes, Cromwell was so impressed with her willingness to suffer in this way on behalf of someone she loved that he dismissed the soldier saying, "Curfew shall not ring tonight."

JAMES S. HEWETT

Ruth's Requirements

When Ruth Bell (later to become Ruth Bell Graham, wife of Billy) left her childhood home in China for schooling in Korea, she wrote the following list of requirements for the perfect husband:

"If I marry: He must be so tall that when he is on his knees, as one has said, he reaches all the way to heaven. His shoulders must be broad enough to bear the burden of a family. His lips must be strong enough to smile, firm enough to say no, and tender enough to kiss. His love must be so deep that it takes its stand in Christ and so wide that it takes the whole lost world in. He must be active enough to save souls. He must be big enough to be gentle and great enough to be thoughtful. His arms must be strong enough to carry a little child."

You have lifted my very soul up to the light of your soul, and I am not ever likely to mistake it for the common daylight.

ELIZABETH BARRETT BROWNING

If there is anything better than to be loved, it is loving.

ANONYMOUS

Love God; love country; love others; love me; but most of all, love.

SMH

Love is a choice that we make. It's an action that we choose to take toward that person we love. You aren't in love; you *do* love.

ROBERT AND ROSEMARY BARNES

A Time to Remind

Remind him you love him when he sees that he has inspired you to greatness.

Emulate his caring concern for others by willingly reaching out to help a neighbor or coworker in distress.

Follow his example of trustworthiness by following through on your promises, calling when you'll be late, letting him know where you'll be if you're not home.

Use him as a role model to strive for excellence in your work, openness in your relationships, and determination in your attempts to solve interpersonal problems.

Let his life be your example of how to have a closer walk with God, a deeper sense of his presence, and a renewed commitment to sharing your witness.

Celebrate his input in your life with a letter of thanks detailing all of the ways his life has been a positive example for you.

People Chow

You will need:

1 small box mixed Chex cereal
1 cup salted pretzels
1 cup peanuts
1 cup mini marshmallows
1 cup raisins
1 cup dried fruit
2 pounds milk chocolate, melted
2 cups powdered sugar
A 2-gallon zippered storage bag

Mix all the dry ingredients in a mixing bowl. Pour the melted chocolate over the mixture and stir in well with a wooden spoon or clean hands. Pour powdered sugar into a 2-gallon zippered storage bag. Add the chocolate mixture to the powdered sugar and shake well until all pieces are covered with sugar. Spread mixture out on waxed paper to cool. Store in an airtight container.

You can deliver this to your sweetheart's office in a decorative tin, with a note that tells him that you're praying for him today.

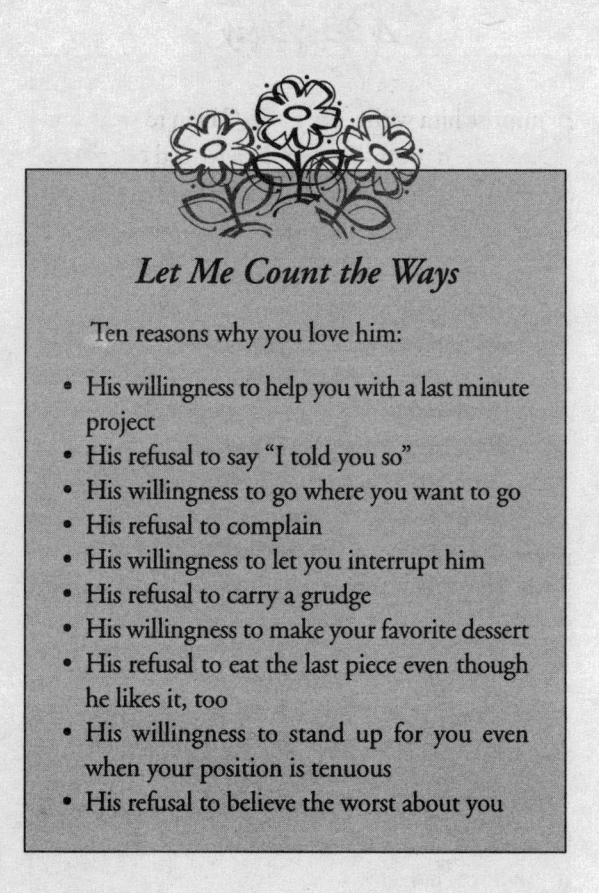

Let Me Count the Ways

Ten reasons why you love him:

- His willingness to help you with a last minute project
- His refusal to say "I told you so"
- His willingness to go where you want to go
- His refusal to complain
- His willingness to let you interrupt him
- His refusal to carry a grudge
- His willingness to make your favorite dessert
- His refusal to eat the last piece even though he likes it, too
- His willingness to stand up for you even when your position is tenuous
- His refusal to believe the worst about you

A Day Away

Surprise him with a day away. Call in to work and take the day off. Turn your pager and cell phone off. Don't consult the clock—just enjoy the day and do what you want to do when you want to do it. Doesn't matter if the day is rainy or bright sunshine—enjoy the day away with each other.

Drive him to his favorite park or nature spot. Go to a car lot and test drive a few cars. Wander through his favorite sporting goods store. Take a cab to a museum or art gallery. Go to an afternoon matinee. Have a leisurely lunch somewhere you've always wanted to go.

Window shop in some expensive downtown stores. Actually wander into a jewelry store and let him try on a few watches and rings. Laugh a lot. Listen a lot. Smile even more.

And when the day is done, linger on the porch and watch the stars come out. He's worth it.

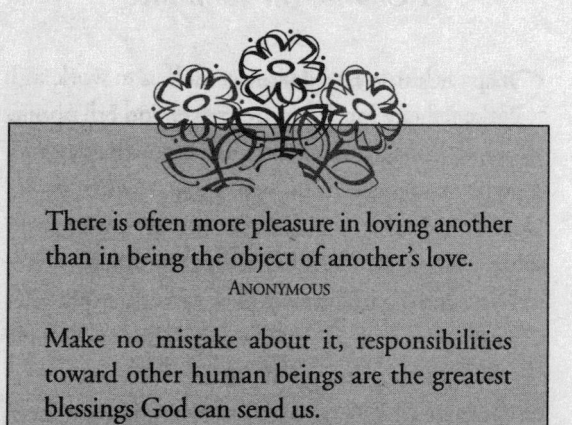

There is often more pleasure in loving another than in being the object of another's love.

ANONYMOUS

Make no mistake about it, responsibilities toward other human beings are the greatest blessings God can send us.

DOROTHY DIX

Romance is a fragile flower, and it cannot long survive where it is ignored or taken for granted. Without commitment and imagination, it will slowly wither and die. But for those who are committed to keeping romance [alive], the best is yet to come.

RICHARD EXLEY

A Chance for Romance

When he's sick, be a doctor of love:

Put together a "hope you feel better" kit. Fill it with tissues, soup mix, cold tablets, aspirin, throat lozenges, a candy or two—Hershey's Kisses® are nice. Include a funny video and some magazines. An inspirational book or favorite novel for reading would be good choices, too.

Offer to run any errands for him that he needs to get done. Call his office to report him as sick. Make sure the cookie jar is filled with his favorite cookies, and that he has snacks whenever he wants them.

Tuck him into bed and let him feel pampered even though he's sick. He'll recover more quickly and will love you for your good bedside manner. When he recovers, he'll tell his friends, too, so be prepared to share with others your tips for treating the sick.

True Love's Example

Knowing the day would be full, he rose early and prayed, as was his custom. After breakfast, he met his friends and greeted them warmly. They laughed and sang and willingly helped people as they walked through town. He loved everyone so much. You could see it. No request was too big or too small for him.

Throughout the day, he kept thinking about how much he loved each one he met. Each thought brought a smile to his face and heart. Yet sometimes other thoughts crowded in on his reverie—thoughts of the hard things he had to face. Those somber reflections cast clouds over his sunny day, but he quickly chased them away by turning his attention to those he loved.

The day progressed with much laughter and love. He chatted amiably with all he met. Finally, early in the evening, he had a quiet supper with his closest friends and then walked to a nearby garden with them to sit and watch the sunset.

The quiet of the garden was shattered by the shouts of angry police. His friends were confused when the police roughly grabbed him and placed him under arrest. Yet he did not fight back. He went with the police to the jailhouse, and there, under the cover of darkness, a trial was held.

Accusers armed with false charges spoke against him, even though he was perfectly innocent. The verdict was swift and sure; he was sentenced to death.

As the sun rose once again over the sleepy town, he was taken to a hillside execution area, wearing a crown of thorns plaited by an onlooker. And, as he was roughly spun around to face the crowd, he spoke aloud his last words:

"Father, forgive them, for they do not know what they are doing."

Indeed, true love follows his example of joy, service, sacrifice, and forgiveness.

MICHAEL HUPP

Jesus said, "Greater love has no one than this, that he lay down his life for his friends."

JOHN 15:13

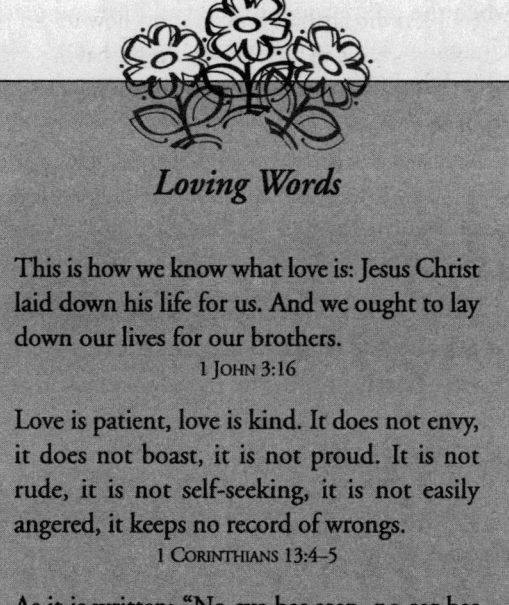

Loving Words

This is how we know what love is: Jesus Christ laid down his life for us. And we ought to lay down our lives for our brothers.
1 JOHN 3:16

Love is patient, love is kind. It does not envy, it does not boast, it is not proud. It is not rude, it is not self-seeking, it is not easily angered, it keeps no record of wrongs.
1 CORINTHIANS 13:4–5

As it is written: "No eye has seen, no ear has heard, no mind has conceived what God has prepared for those who love him."
1 CORINTHIANS 2:9

May your unfailing love rest upon us, O LORD, even as we put our hope in you.
PSALM 33:22

Great Dates

Couples who are best friends know how to put the sparkle back in their love life by having great dates. Here are a few suggestions of some dates you could try.

A Photo Date: Purchase a disposable camera. Go to your favorite haunts and start snapping away. Ask a bystander to take your picture together. Keep snapping until all of the shots are used. Drop the camera at a one-hour developing place and share a cup of cocoa until the pictures are ready.

Too-Tired Date: Put on your most comfy loungewear. Order takeout food, turn on the answering machine, and just relax in front of a favorite video or snuggled together on the couch with copies of your favorite books.

Gourmet Cooking Date: Plan the menu, do the grocery shopping together at an upscale market, and cook your dinner together! Experiment with new ideas and menu items. Bon appetit!

DAVID AND CLAUDIA ARP

Loving Him

Use this page to record your feelings about your love for him:

_____

_____

_____

_____

_____

_____

_____

_____

_____

_____

_____

_____

_____

_____

_____

_____

_____

_____

Love tugs on heart strings and ties two lives into one with a special knot.
GAY TALBOTT BOASSY

Love is the only service that power cannot command and money cannot buy.
ANONYMOUS

Connecting at the level of the head will get the task done, but only by connecting our hearts to each other can we become the intimate soul mates of our dreams.
PATRICK M. MORLEY

Love is the master key that opens the gates of happiness.
OLIVER WENDELL HOLMES

True love is like an overflowing fountain—it touches everyone who passes by.
SMH

Let Me Count the Ways

Ten reasons you love him like you do:

- He shows you respect
- He shows you kindness
- He shows you trust
- He shows you mercy
- He shows you tenderheartedness
- He shows you appreciation
- He shows you true friendship
- He shows you gentleness
- He shows you faithfulness
- He shows you loving concern

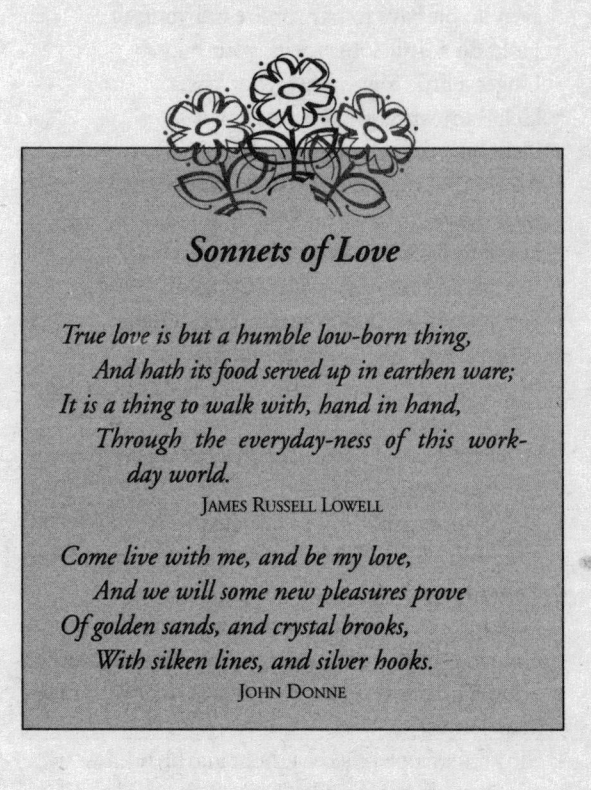

Sonnets of Love

True love is but a humble low-born thing,
*   And hath its food served up in earthen ware;*
It is a thing to walk with, hand in hand,
*   Through the everyday-ness of this work-*
*   day world.*
JAMES RUSSELL LOWELL

Come live with me, and be my love,
*   And we will some new pleasures prove*
Of golden sands, and crystal brooks,
*   With silken lines, and silver hooks.*
JOHN DONNE

- Call him every day when you're on a business trip even if you have to pay for the call yourself.
- Hold on a little longer with your hugs.
- Linger a little longer with your kisses.
- Help him write his life's story.
- Help him find ways to simplify his life.
- Accept that his strengths most probably will be your weaknesses.
- Learn to Rollerblade together.
- Buy him a pint of gourmet ice cream.
- Forgive any grudges you may be carrying.
- Surprise him with a candlelight dinner.
- Make him a wreath for his office door out of Hershey's Kisses®.
- Purchase a dated Christmas tree ornament for your fifth anniversary.
- Help him organize his old photos.
- Give him the gift of time by doing some of his chores for him.
- Give him a coupon for a soft ice cream cone at the Dairy Queen®—to be redeemed anytime he wants it.
- Leave a love note on the refrigerator door with magnetic letters.
- Slip a foil wrapped chocolate heart into his briefcase with a note attached that reads: "You've stolen my heart."
- Give him a coupon for breakfast in bed that can be redeemed this month.
- Wrap up a package of golf tees in a gift box along with your offer to play mini golf the following weekend.
- Treat him as if he were Prince Charming.

Love N Cents

Here are ten inexpensive ways to show and share your love:

- Play on a playground swing set together.
- Ride a merry-go-round at the fair together.
- Splash through rain puddles together.
- Go sled riding together in the park.
- Go to pick a pumpkin in a farmer's pumpkin patch together.
- Harvest a bumper crop of sweet cherries together.
- Attend an outdoor art festival together.
- Go on a lazy boat or canoe ride on a pond together.
- Shout out your love into a canyon or valley and listen for the echo.
- Sing in the rain together.

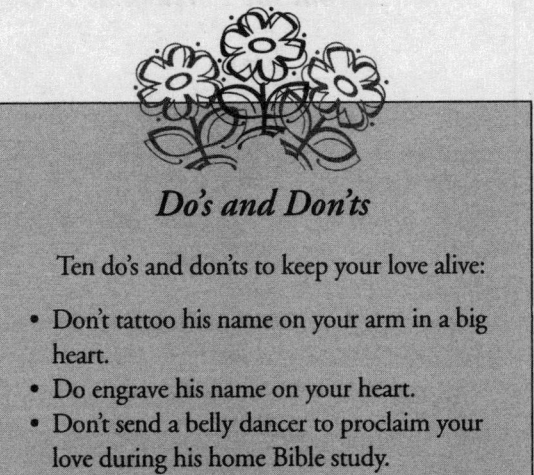

Do's and Don'ts

Ten do's and don'ts to keep your love alive:

- Don't tattoo his name on your arm in a big heart.
- Do engrave his name on your heart.
- Don't send a belly dancer to proclaim your love during his home Bible study.
- Do hide a bookmark in his Bible that tells him how much you love him.
- Don't toast your love with a glass of prune juice.
- Do toast your love with his favorite sparkling beverage.
- Don't call him an old boyfriend's nickname.
- Do give him a special name that only you two know.
- Don't talk about another fellow to make him jealous.
- Do give him all of your love and affection—always.

Sonnets from the Portuguese XXI

Say over again, and yet once over "again,"
That thou dost love me. Though the word repeated
Should seem 'a cuckoo-song,' as thou dost treat it,
Remember, never to the hill or plain,
Valley and wood, without her cuckoo-strain,
Comes the fresh Spring in all her green completed.
Beloved, I, amid the darkness greeted
By a doubtful spirit-voice, in that doubt's pain
Cry, 'Speak once more—thou lovest!' Who can fear
Too many stars, though each in heaven shall roll—
Too many flowers, though each shall crown the year?
Say thou dost love me, love me, love me—toll
The silver iterance!—only minding, Dear,
To love me also in silence, with thy soul.

ELIZABETH BARRETT BROWNING

Tiger Butter

You will need:

1 pound of milk chocolate
½ pound of white chocolate
½ pound of creamy peanut butter

Melt each ingredient separately and keep them warm, being careful not to burn them. Mix the white chocolate with the peanut butter. Spread this mixture onto a cookie sheet that has been lined with waxed paper. Swirl the melted milk chocolate onto the peanut mixture, drawing a knife back and forth through the mixture until the chocolate and peanut butter resemble tiger stripes. Allow the candy to harden. Break into bite-sized pieces and store in an airtight container.

Serve this treat with a note that tells him that he's as strong as a tiger, but as gentle as a pussy cat. Seal the treat with a hug.

- Keep a photo at work of the man you love. If possible, keep it where you will see it several times a day.
- Send him a love letter every day the week before your anniversary.
- Plant a rosebush, a tree, or some other long-lived garden plant that symbolizes your long-lasting commitment to each other.
- Write a letter to him telling him why you would want to meet him and get to know him all over again.
- Make him a Christmas stocking from fabric scraps— sew it all by yourself (ask a neighbor to help if you've never sewn anything before).
- Realize that he may see the gift of a work bench for the garage as an appropriate anniversary present.
- Let him use your best skillet.
- Don't criticize his barbeque skills even if he burns the burgers.
- Never, never, never take him for granted.
- Enjoy his company.
- Make reservations for that fishing getaway he's been telling you about.
- Believe him when he says you're terrific.
- Make a list of all the wonderful things that have happened in your life since you've known him.
- Take him for a ride in a hot air balloon.
- Donate a book to the public library in his honor.
- Ask if you can help him organize the CDs and videos.
- Set aside one evening a month for a game night. Play what he wants to play.
- Never try to teach him to use a sewing machine or computer.

A Time to Remind

Take time to remind him how much you love him by arranging a formal "Dinner in the Park" date. Dress up in your best evening wear—black tie and formal evening gown. Grab a picnic basket and head for a quiet spot in a city park or on a bluff overlooking the lights of the city. Don't bother with folding chairs. A good-sized blanket spread on the ground will protect your clothing and give you a comfortable place for your alfresco dinner.

Bring along a battery operated cassette or CD player and play quiet mood music as you enjoy your night under the stars. Better yet, consult your local paper to see if an outdoor concert may be scheduled nearby and include that in your "Dinner in the Park" date. End the evening by making a wish together on a star for many more wonderful evenings to come.

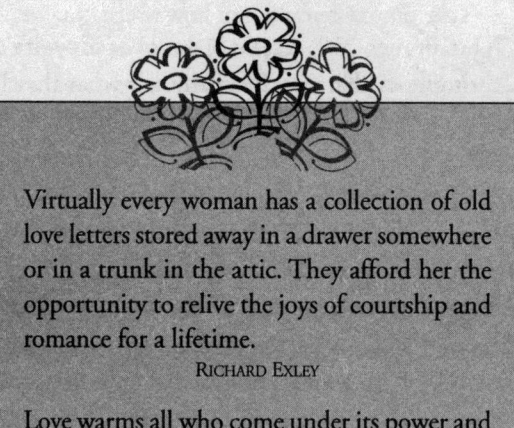

Virtually every woman has a collection of old love letters stored away in a drawer somewhere or in a trunk in the attic. They afford her the opportunity to relive the joys of courtship and romance for a lifetime.

RICHARD EXLEY

Love warms all who come under its power and lightens all hearts who yield to its influence.

SMH

Love is being willing to face risks to see your spouse's dreams come true.

Mud, Denim, and Chocolates

Certain men pick certain boxes of candy—it's a simple as that. I can usually tell what they'll pick as soon as they enter the store and head for the candy rack. A mystery man dressed in denim shoved his big, rough hands into his pockets and paraded up and down the aisle in front of the candy before finally choosing one.

Nope, I thought to myself. That one's not right for you. It's too little. As if he heard what I was thinking, he replaced it and reached for another.

Still not right, I thought. Too gaudy. This man was many things, but gaudy he was not. I didn't think his sweetheart would be either. He soon tossed that one aside as well and reached for the third one.

I smiled. He held it in his left hand while examining a more decorated one with a plastic rose and ribbon. No, I thought again. Stop while you're ahead.

Finally, he made his decision. He laid the rose-topped box down and proceeded to the cash register with the simpler but more elegant box of candy. He left the store while I paid for my purchases.

I noticed the big man in denim standing near the back of a pickup truck that looked as if it had been dipped in mud and oven baked. I continued to stand there out of sheer amazement and disbelief. The big man dressed in denim and wearing muddy boots peeled the cellophane wrapper, removed the lid, and lovingly fed his elegant box of Valentine candy to his hunting dog.

GAIL L. ROBERSON

Love and Laughter

Make this a loving, laughter-filled day for him. Here are some suggestions to get you started:

Send him a funny e-mail.

Recall a time when something embarrassing happened. Can you laugh about it now with him?

Copy three or four jokes from a joke book and hide them in his toolbox. Next time he goes looking for a screwdriver, he'll find a laugh instead.

Pop a humor cassette or CD in his car stereo system so that he will have something to laugh about on his way to work.

Recall a time when you were surprised by happiness or laughter. Share a story about that time with him.

Leave a joke or funny comic on the mirror.

Smile a silly smile and make him laugh.

Talk about the favorite places you have lived or visited that really made you smile.

Look for ways to take yourself less seriously. Play with little children's toys at an adult dinner party, have a water balloon fight, challenge each other to design a wacky hat—and wear it out to a restaurant!

Serve supper backwards—give him his dessert first and end with a salad. Act as if nothing is out of the ordinary, and watch the smiles begin.

A Chance for Romance

Find a chance for romance by having a "left over" party. If you have children, send them to a babysitter or friend's house for the evening. The one rule is, you may not cook anything new—the meal must consist of what's sitting in the back of the refrigerator. (As long as it hasn't already turned into a science experiment!) Tablespoons of stuff are allowed and encouraged.

Make sure the oven is warm or a microwave is available to re-warm everything. Any leftovers not consumed after dinner go to the dog or disposal! Use paper plates so that there are no dishes to wash.

Limit the evening's conversation topics: no politics, finances, work, family or children problems, and no religious discussions. (That leaves little to talk about except sex, love, and laughter!) At the end of the evening, cuddle on the couch with a leftover dessert and top off the event with a Kool-aid toast! And seal the toast with a kiss.

The Mystery of Love

Keeping a healthy, growing relationship requires friendship, fun and romance. And there's nothing like a mystery date to encourage all of these facets of love to flower and grow.

Start now to plan your mystery date. Keep the destination and arrangements secret for as long as possible. Allow guessing, but don't reveal too much with your answers. After all, this date is a mystery! You might even want to blindfold your sweetheart until you've reached your final destination and have him try to guess where you're going by the sounds and smells along the way.

The date might include a concert, a favorite or new restaurant, or even a surprise getaway. But don't over-schedule your date. Be sure to include some time for communicating and reviving the spark that brought you two together in the first place.

- Keep a definition of love in the calendar you carry around to help keep your life in a loving perspective.
- Let him invite his friends over for a Super Bowl party; offer to serve snacks and clean up.
- Give hugs when the day has been especially tough for him—and when it has been especially easy, too!
- Rent a convertible and take a leisurely drive until the stars come out.
- Exercise and stay in shape together.
- Rock in a double rocker on the screened porch, holding hands.
- Sleep outside on a balcony under the stars.
- Secretly pass a love note to him during a serious budget meeting at church.
- While riding in an elevator, tell him he looks wonderful.
- Issue him a coupon entitling him to one hour of cuddling in a location of his choice.
- Give yourself permission to be sexy.
- Don't let one day go by without telling him how handsome he is.
- Be aware of current events and concerned enough to talk about these things with him.
- Keep yourself healthy.
- Sharpen all of his pencils.
- Remember to replace the roll of toilet paper if you were the last one to use it up.
- Never return his car without gasoline.
- Give him extra kisses for checking your car's oil and tire pressure.
- Accept his offer to help fold the laundry even if he may not do it exactly as you would like.

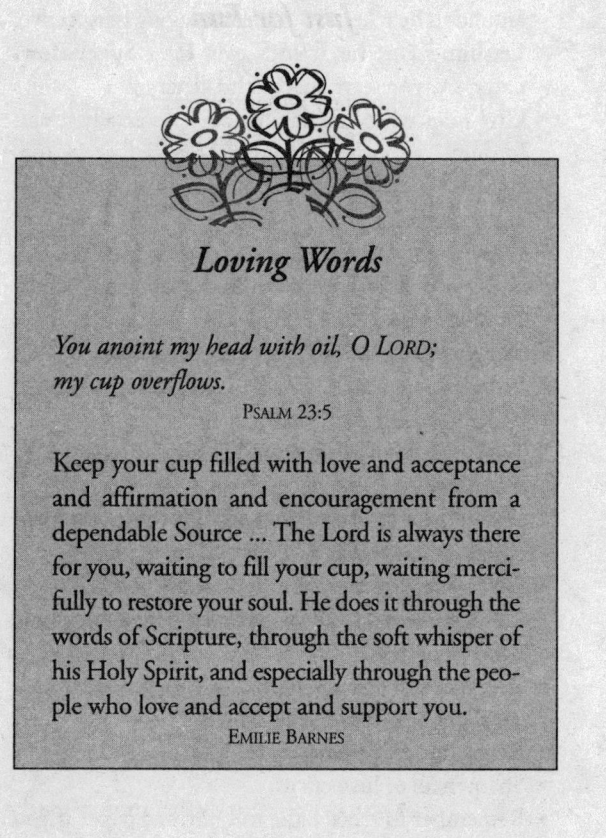

Loving Words

You anoint my head with oil, O LORD;
my cup overflows.

PSALM 23:5

Keep your cup filled with love and acceptance
and affirmation and encouragement from a
dependable Source ... The Lord is always there
for you, waiting to fill your cup, waiting merci-
fully to restore your soul. He does it through the
words of Scripture, through the soft whisper of
his Holy Spirit, and especially through the people who love and accept and support you.

EMILIE BARNES

Just for Fun

To keep the mystery and interest alive in your relationship, why not try one or two of these dating ideas—just for fun!

Go out for a drive on the back roads. See if you can get lost and then find your way home again. If you know the area too well, try driving in one direction for three minutes and then change direction at the next crossroads and drive for another three minutes. Continue this process for an hour. You'll probably see some territory you've never seen before. Stop along the way and grab a snack at a new restaurant. The only problem is, if you like the restaurant, you may never be able to find it again!

Send him a mysterious "treasure map" to lead him to a secret rendezvous. Have a meal planned and something to do, too, like a game of mini golf, a concert, or a stroll by a stream when he finally finds you.

Go sailing in a small sailboat on a nearby lake. Rent a wave runner if you prefer something noisier and faster, or try a small boat with an outboard motor. Find a secluded spot along shore and enjoy some time just sitting and watching the water.

A Time to Remind

Take time to remind him you love him when you look into the future with him. No one can predict what will happen to any of us over the next decade. So, why not make a time capsule that incorporates some of the essence of who you two are right now in this place in your relationship. Record your values, your church, your history together, and how you met. Include recent photos of yourselves and a description of your most treasured possession. Write down a testimony of your personal faith, too. Then list some goals and dreams and plans that the two of you share.

Bury your time capsule in a corner of the backyard, behind a loose brick in the basement, underneath a pile of junk in the attic, or any other place where it will remain undisturbed for some time. Then give each other a kiss, knowing that you've left your mark of love on the world.

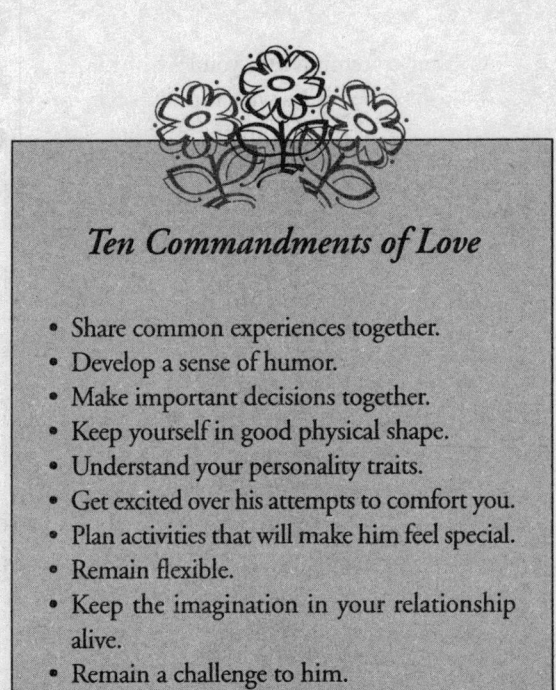

Ten Commandments of Love

- Share common experiences together.
- Develop a sense of humor.
- Make important decisions together.
- Keep yourself in good physical shape.
- Understand your personality traits.
- Get excited over his attempts to comfort you.
- Plan activities that will make him feel special.
- Remain flexible.
- Keep the imagination in your relationship alive.
- Remain a challenge to him.

GARY SMALLEY

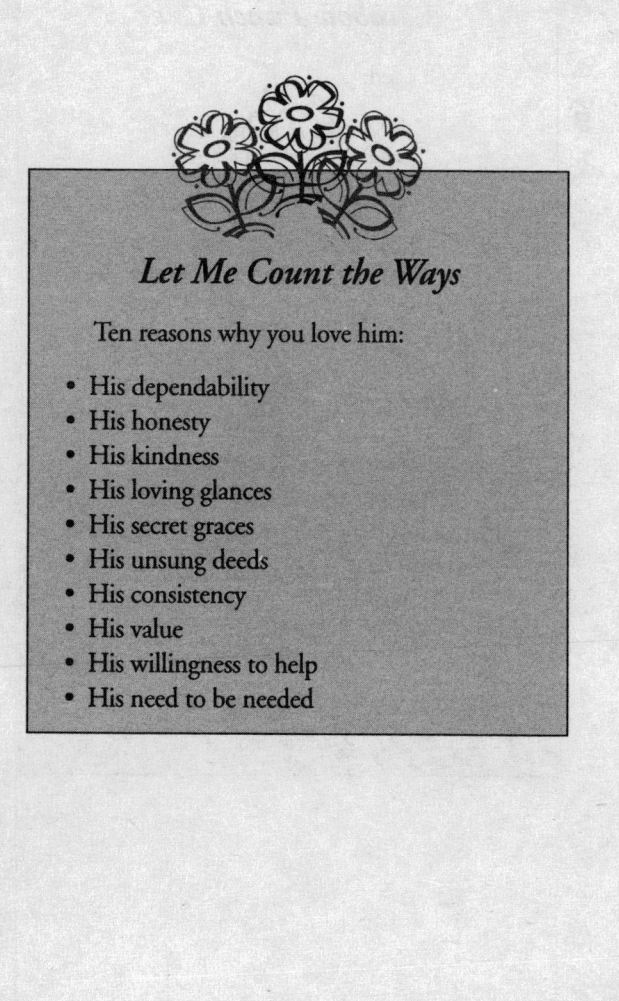

Let Me Count the Ways

Ten reasons why you love him:

- His dependability
- His honesty
- His kindness
- His loving glances
- His secret graces
- His unsung deeds
- His consistency
- His value
- His willingness to help
- His need to be needed

Rainbow Punch Cake

You will need:

An angel food cake in a ring shape
Whipped topping
Chocolate candy coins
Three pans or bowls of three different colors of
    prepared Jell-O
OR
Jell-O handi-snacks in three different flavors

Slice off about 1 inch of the top of the angel food cake ring. Save this top for use at the end of the recipe. Hollow out the remainder of the cake. Discard. Fill hollowed out cake with cubes or spoonfuls of different colored Jell-O. Replace the top of the cake, and ice the cake with the whipped topping. Sprinkle chocolate coins on the top and sides of the cake.

Include a note with the cake that says, "You are my treasure at the end of the rainbow."

The Language of Love

I've learned the Lord's language of love. When I tell Jesus that I love him, it has nothing to do with romance. But passion? Yes! My love for Jesus is not a syrupy sentiment, but it is definitely zealous and fervent, spirited and intense. When I praise him, I want the melody to come right from my heart.

And this is the way we are to love our brothers and sisters. Throw your caution to the wind and invite the Spirit of God to fill your heart with the warmth and passion of praise. And love others with the same warmth and affection you reserve for him.

JONI EARECKSON TADA

How can you share this new insight with the one you love? Does he know the Lord's language of love?

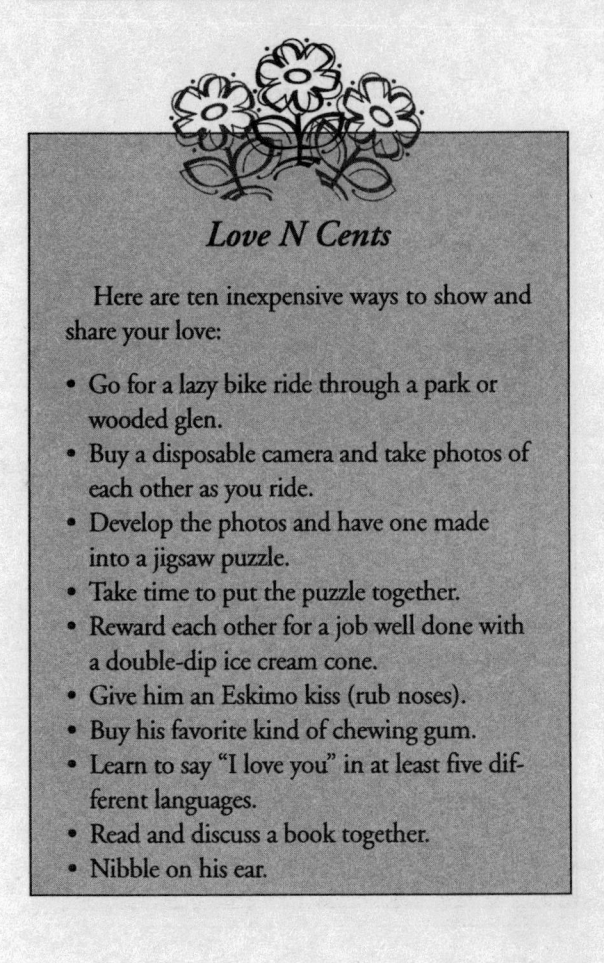

Love N Cents

Here are ten inexpensive ways to show and share your love:

- Go for a lazy bike ride through a park or wooded glen.
- Buy a disposable camera and take photos of each other as you ride.
- Develop the photos and have one made into a jigsaw puzzle.
- Take time to put the puzzle together.
- Reward each other for a job well done with a double-dip ice cream cone.
- Give him an Eskimo kiss (rub noses).
- Buy his favorite kind of chewing gum.
- Learn to say "I love you" in at least five different languages.
- Read and discuss a book together.
- Nibble on his ear.

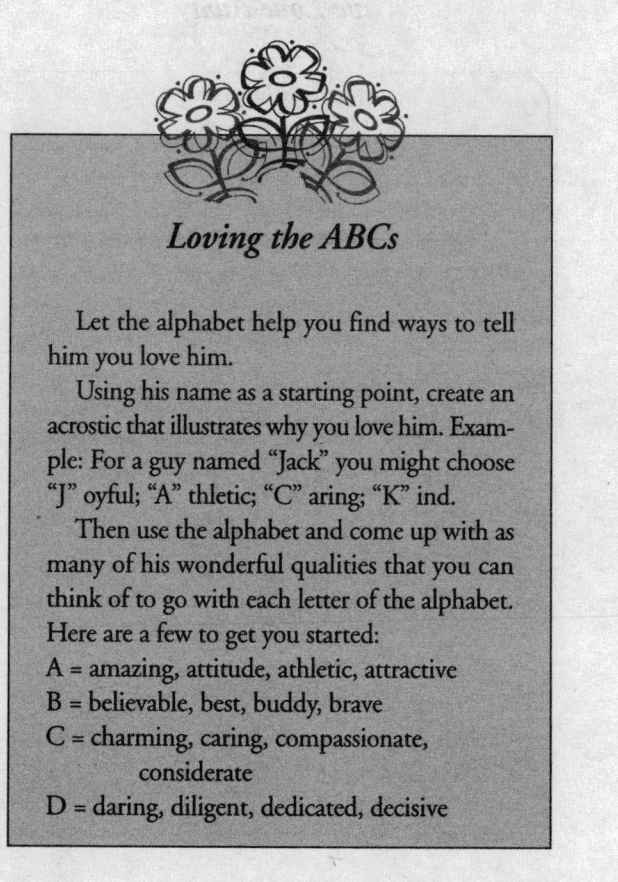

Loving the ABCs

Let the alphabet help you find ways to tell him you love him.

Using his name as a starting point, create an acrostic that illustrates why you love him. Example: For a guy named "Jack" you might choose "J" oyful; "A" thletic; "C" aring; "K" ind.

Then use the alphabet and come up with as many of his wonderful qualities that you can think of to go with each letter of the alphabet. Here are a few to get you started:

A = amazing, attitude, athletic, attractive
B = believable, best, buddy, brave
C = charming, caring, compassionate, considerate
D = daring, diligent, dedicated, decisive

Give Love Away

One evening just before the great Broadway musical star Mary Martin was to go on stage in *South Pacific*, a note was handed to her. It was from Oscar Hammerstein, who at that moment was on his deathbed. The short note simply said:

"Dear Mary, A bell's not a bell till you ring it. A song's not a song till you sing it. Love in your heart is not put there to stay. Love isn't love till you give it away."

After her performance that night many people rushed backstage, crying, "Mary, what happened to you out there tonight? We never saw anything like that performance before."

Blinking back the tears, Mary then read them the note from Hammerstein. Then she said, "Tonight, I gave my love away!"

JAMES S. HEWETT

- Learn to sing an Italian love song.
- Touch each other often by giving hugs every chance you get.
- Unconditionally accept each other.
- Agree to never tickle his super sensitive feet.
- Stare deeply into his eyes and see your love reflected back to you.
- Give him the freedom to be different.
- Recognize your need for growth and change.
- Compromise cheerfully when necessary.
- Let him operate in his areas of strength.
- Learn from him.
- Always do for him what you would want him to do for you.
- Send him a romantic e-mail message several times a week.
- Call if you're running late.
- Learn to tap out "I love you" in Morse code.
- Bake him a birthday cake in the shape of his favorite piece of sporting equipment.
- Keep extra batteries around for his electronic gadgets and gizmos.
- Spray your signature perfume in his car.
- Be a mentor to a young woman and show her how a lady should be treated by the way your man treats you!
- Light a fire in the fireplace and read love poems to him.
- Offer to help him carry some of his things (packages, briefcase, bowling bag, etc.) instead of walking empty handed.

A Program for Happiness

To live content with small means;
To seek elegance rather than luxury,
and refinement rather than fashion;
To be worthy, not respectable,
and wealthy, not rich;
To study hard, think quietly,
talk gently, act frankly;
To listen to stars and birds,
to babes and sages, with open heart;
To bear all cheerfully, do all bravely,
await occasions, hurry never.
In a word, to let the spiritual, unbidden and
    unconscious,
grow up through the common.

WILLIAM HENRY CHANNING

A Time to Remind

Take time to remind him you love him when you bring a carryout dinner home in an unusual way. It may take a little planning, but the extra effort will be worth it.

Purchase boxes or tins in graduated sizes. Line each box or tin with a zippered storage bag. Order his favorite Chinese, Thai, Italian, or Greek meal. Place each dinner item in a separate container. Stack the containers in order of size with the largest one on the bottom. Tie them all together with a colorful, wide ribbon and a big floppy bow.

Deliver the stacked containers with a folded towel on your arm and a twinkle in your eye. The smile on his face will make the meal taste even better than it looks.

A wise lover values not so much the gift of the lover as the love of the giver.

THOMAS À KEMPIS

Love is not a matter of counting the years; it is making the years count.

WILLIAM SMITH

Love grows of its own free will; it cannot be commanded.

UNKNOWN

Clear knowledge is the parent of love; wisdom, love itself.

AUGUSTUS HARE

The heart is a lamp with just oil enough to burn for an hour, and if there be no oil to put in again, its light will go out. God's grace is the oil that fills the lamp of love.

HENRY WARD BEECHER

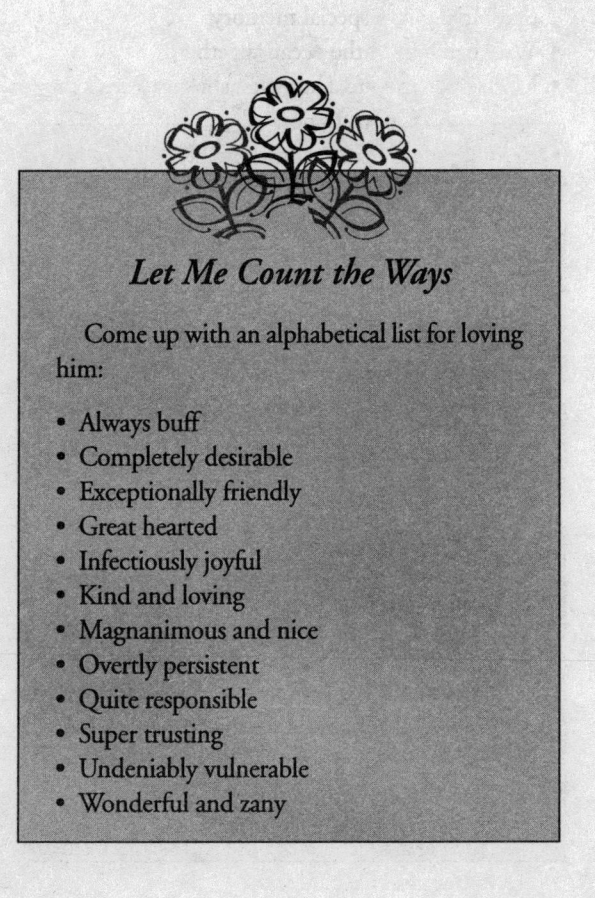

Let Me Count the Ways

Come up with an alphabetical list for loving him:

- Always buff
- Completely desirable
- Exceptionally friendly
- Great hearted
- Infectiously joyful
- Kind and loving
- Magnanimous and nice
- Overtly persistent
- Quite responsible
- Super trusting
- Undeniably vulnerable
- Wonderful and zany

- Give your beloved a Christmas ornament each year that highlights a special memory.
- Walk barefoot in the ocean together.
- Make a donation to a homeless shelter or crisis pregnancy center in his honor.
- Remind yourself every day how blessed you are to have him in your life.
- Let something he did wrong go without comment.
- Place a single red rose in his briefcase.
- When apart, think about each other for one minute at a pre-determined time.
- Believe that the best is yet to come.
- Learn the sign language signal for "I love you."
- Give away that ugly frilly couch that you know he can't stand and that isn't really all that comfortable anyway.
- Let him keep his uncle's old Victorian clock on the desk even though it doesn't work.
- Don't send his uncle's old Victorian clock out to be fixed unless you ask him first.
- Go with him to see his favorite action/adventure movie.
- Buy him his favorite snacks to eat during a movie or concert.
- Find out where the pro teams hold their training camps and take him unexpectedly.
- Buy a box of sparklers and set them off on his birthday.
- Never mention his bald spot.
- Buy him season tickets to his favorite sport with a companion ticket for you.
- Share an inside joke that only he will understand.

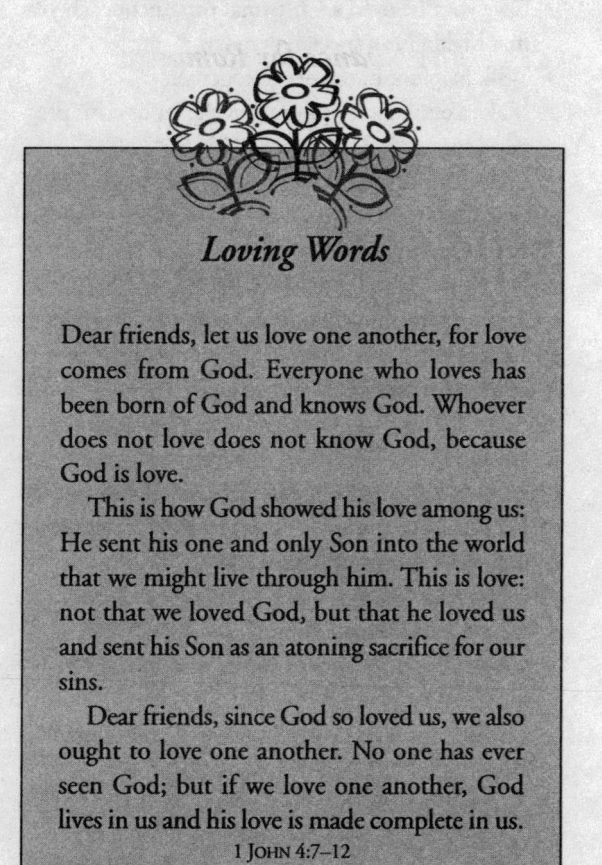

Loving Words

Dear friends, let us love one another, for love comes from God. Everyone who loves has been born of God and knows God. Whoever does not love does not know God, because God is love.

This is how God showed his love among us: He sent his one and only Son into the world that we might live through him. This is love: not that we loved God, but that he loved us and sent his Son as an atoning sacrifice for our sins.

Dear friends, since God so loved us, we also ought to love one another. No one has ever seen God; but if we love one another, God lives in us and his love is made complete in us.

1 JOHN 4:7–12

A Chance for Romance

A year of doing, caring, loving, sharing, growing, and being together involves many opportunities for romance. Remember to set aside a time once a year to get away and reconnect with each other.

Maybe you would prefer to go to a mountain cabin, seaside condo, or a woodland tent. Maybe you'd prefer something a little different like a penthouse suite, an old style hotel, or a cozy bed and breakfast. Wherever you choose to go, make sure you have no set schedule. Allow yourselves plenty of time to sit by the fire. Take long walks. Share your hopes and dreams. Renew your commitment to each other. Review what has happened this year and where you'd like to be in your relationship next year.

Set goals, and dream dreams of togetherness. By the time you head back home, you'll be relaxed, refreshed, renewed and more in love with each other than when you arrived. This is one chance for romance you don't want to let slip by.

Going my way of old,
Contented more or less,
I dreamt not life could hold
Such happiness.
I dreamt not that love's way
Could keep the golden height
Day after happy day,
Night after night.

WILFRED WILSON GIBSON

Young and in love—how magical the phrase!
How magical the fact! Who has not yearned
Over young lovers when to their amaze
They fall in love, and find their love returned,
And the lights brighten, and their eyes are clear
To see God's image in their common clay.
Is it the music of the spheres they hear!
Is it the prelude to that noble play
The drama of Joined Lives?

ALICE DUER MILLER